Acclaim for: *The Optimistic Jew*

"Tsvi Bisk presents a comprehensive critique of where the Jewish people are at the beginning of the 21st century, how we got here and where we should be going if we want to not only survive but also to flourish. *The Optimistic Jew* is original and iconoclastic. It deals with reality and not ideological wishful thinking. But it is also an idealistic book that presents a positive, even heroic, vision of what the Jewish future could be if we choose to apply our rational faculties to the new global reality. The book challenges inherited assumptions and presents a framework for positive action. It should become a primary reference for Jewish policymakers."

Gad Yaacobi, former Israeli Ambassador to the United Nations and Cabinet Minister in Israeli Governments.

"Few writers can match Bisk in his in-depth grasp of the situation of world Jewry yesterday, today, and tomorrow. Few have the creativity, the sensitivity, and the chutzpah to make spirit-stretching sense of it. Few are as helpful in enabling us to feel the urgency of the situation, know how high are the stakes, and resolve to do more to assure a 21st century for world Jewry that honors us all, Jew and Gentile alike."

Professor Arthur B. Shostak Sociologist Drexel University, Philadelphia, PA

"At a time of rising anti-Semitism, nuclear proliferation, stagnant peace process and open calls by Muslim leaders for the destruction of Israel many predict a gloomy future for the Jewish people. Tsvi Bisk is not one of them. In this thoughtful and compelling book Bisk argues that the 21st Century offers a bright future for the Jewish people and many opportunities for them to excel in an increasingly globalized world. This book is a wonderful antidote for Jewish fatalism."

Dr. Gal Luft, Executive Director, Institute for the Analysis of Global Security, Washington D.C.

"Tsvi Bisk is one of the most innovative thinkers about the future, the Jewish people, and the interaction between them. Bisk combines the best of the futurist and the visionary – able not only to understand what the future might hold, but also embracing that future with a sense of opportunity, rather than one of fear and denial. Bisk has a gift for courageous imagination. He is a provocative and lucid thinker who challenges our existing frames of thought and encourages us to see the benefit in adopting new modes of thinking. Above all, Bisk contributes to the ability of the Jewish people to actively improve their future, rather than sit passively by as a new wave of change washes over. This is a book which every person who wishes to be a leader of the Jewish people, or of some Jewish people, in 2020 should read."

Einat Wilf, Author of *My Israel, Our Generation*; co-founder of *Kol Dor*

"This book has made me again proud to be a Jew after years of despair of Israel and the Jewish people. Bisk opens a new realm of identity for me as a Jew and a Zionist."

William Cohen, Data Management Consultant, Tel Aviv

THE
OPTIMISTIC
JEW

A Positive Vision for the Jewish People in the 21st Century

Tsvi Bisk

MAXANNA PRESS

2007, Israel

Published by
Maxanna Press
a division of
Ziv Group Ltd.
46 B/4 Jerusalem St
Kfar Saba, Israel 44369
info@zivgroup.co.il

Cover Design by Ruhama Shaulsky

ATTENTION organizations, synagogues, schools, Jewish studies programs, reading clubs, mission/conference organizers, birthright programs etc.: Bulk orders for fundraisers, premiums or gifts can earn a 40-60% discount on retail price (according to number of books ordered). Please contact the publisher at info@zivgroup.co.il

Maxanna is a registered trademark of Ziv Group Ltd.

ISBN: 978-1-934515-72-3

Printed in Israel

10 9 8 7 6 5 4 3 2 1

FOR MY FRIENDS
Micaela Ziv
&
Bill Cohen

Their encouragement and support
enabled me to write this book.

WHY YOU SHOULD READ THIS BOOK

The purpose of this book is to stimulate imagination and activate energy and idealism in a Jewish context. The seeds of the positive future envisioned here are already germinating in numerous projects initiated by young Israelis and Diaspora Jews who want something more from their Jewish identity. It is my hope that the ideas suggested will help stimulate the development of a 21st century Jewish paradigm as compelling as the 20th century Jewish paradigm which created the State of Israel and the extraordinary institutional structure of Diaspora Jewry.

This paradigm succeeded beyond its creators' wildest expectations. But for many young Jews it is no longer adequate to their needs and ambitions as they confront the reality of the 21st century. For many it is no longer attractive or compelling.

Yet I am *The Optimistic Jew*. I believe we have the capability to reinvent ourselves and build a wonderful new Jewish paradigm. The core theme of the book is that the global reality of the 21st century at last provides Israel and the Diaspora with the means to enable the self-actualization of the Jewish individual.

HOW YOU SHOULD READ THIS BOOK

The book is divided into two parts.

Part I – Where We Are and Where We Should be Going is an analysis of the Jewish present.

Part II – Realization: Looking Back From 2020 is an imagineered but plausible future looking back from the vantage point of the year 2020. It demonstrates how the Jewish people and Israel will have confronted the challenges and achieved the aims outlined in Part I.

The book has been organized in a certain manner and the chapters logically follow one another. While it would be beneficial to read the book in the order presented, each chapter can also be read as an independent essay. And while the second part obviously draws from the first part, it too can be read independently. The well informed reader might even want to begin with Part II. In any case, readers should feel free to treat the book as if it were a buffet and "jump in" at any point, reading forward or backward (or both) as they wish.

I wrote this book with the intent to engage a certain Jewish reading public. Because of this I welcome discussion and feedback and invite you to contact me at bisk@zivgroup.co.il. Please also visit our website: www.theoptimisticjew.com.

TABLE OF CONTENTS

Why you should read this book
How you should read this book

Part I – Where We Are and Where We Should Be Going

Part II – Realization: Looking Back From 2020

"It often happens that the universal belief of one age, a belief from which no one could be free without extraordinary effort of genius or courage, becomes to a subsequent one so palpable an absurdity that the only difficulty is, to imagine how such an idea could ever have appeared credible."

John Stuart Mill

| PART I |

WHERE WE ARE AND WHERE WE SHOULD BE GOING

Jewish life in the 21st century must:
- mobilize and direct the energies of the Jewish people into practical and creative activity as intense as the pre and early state eras,
- transform Israel into a society with the highest possible scientific, cultural, and social standards,
- turn Israel into an economic super power with one of the highest per capita standards of living in the world,
- enlist the abilities of the *entire* Jewish people to create new frameworks and services geared to answering vital world needs in the 21st century.

Israel must become the tool of Jewish civilization not its aim. Jews do not exist for Israel; Israel exists for the Jews. Our national visions must evolve into national-universal visions with national-universal obligations for a national-universal people. Unless we develop a new national-universal paradigm of Jewish existence we will fail to develop the instruments necessary for *particular* Jewish existence in the 21st century. Israel cannot truly become a Jewish center unless it becomes a world center and conversely, it cannot become a world center unless it becomes a Jewish center.

At present Israel is often perceived to be part of the problem not part of the solution. Becoming part of the solution would strengthen Israel's international position and world Jewry in general. It would also:

- excite the imagination of young Jews around the world,
- provide them with concrete frameworks in which to express their idealism and apply their abilities,
- solve many social problems now plaguing Israel and the world.

| INTRODUCTION |

THE BACKGROUND TO OPTIMISM

Why am I optimistic about the future of the Jews? Because the "flat (globalized) world" that Tom Friedman describes in his book *The World is Flat* enables the Jewish People to turn the 21st century into the century in which one's Jewishness will no longer be a burden or barrier, or constitute a sacrifice. This could be the century in which Jews as individuals will be able to realize their human potential without sacrificing Jewish ambitions and realize their Jewish potential without sacrificing their human ambitions. No people on earth are better prepared by virtue of education, temperament, and historical adaptability to embrace the challenges of the 21st century. Two thousand years of prevailing in the face of constant discrimination have prepared the Jews, perhaps more than any other people, to take advantage of the opportunities of this globalized world. Never before have we lived in an era so amenable to our temperament and our survival skills.

To do this we must free ourselves of certain attitudes that have become a barrier to taking advantage of the opportunities of the 21st century. First and foremost we must stop making a fetish of past suffering and focus on creating a Jewish future based on our relative advantages. Classical Zionism sought to use the past as an inspiration to build a better future. This is what made Israel and its early social experiments so attractive for Jews and non-Jews alike until the 6 Day War. Today, however, it seems that many Diaspora and Israeli Jews fear the future and use the past, not as an inspiration, but as an excuse not to deal with the future. As a consequence Israel and Jewish identity have become less attractive. The rise of post-Zionism in Israel and declining identification with Jewish issues among young Diaspora Jews are indications of this.

We seem unable to understand that the technological and political developments of globalization will affect our efforts to sustain a meaningful Jewish society in the 21st century. Many problems that presently agitate Israel and world Jewry derive from our inability to reevaluate our circumstances in light of these developments. To properly address the problems we face we must acknowledge two self-evident truths: first that *the Jews have always been part of world developments* and, second that *the future is always more important than the past.*

We must rid ourselves of the "Nation that Dwells Alone" attitude. This attitude is founded on historical apprehensions that are real. But this does not release us from the responsibility of recognizing the realities and opportunities of the 21st century. The Jews are part of the human race; we do not "dwell alone". The misuse of this term by political and spiritual populists in order to suggest that the Jews can and even must ignore historical trends that affect all humanity is a recipe for self-destruction.

THE DILEMMA OF THE PAST

To understand the proper relationship between the past and the future we would do well to refer to David Ben-Gurion who once remarked that the past 1,000 years of Jewish history were important but that the next 1,000 years are more important. This reflects an outlook that the past, with all its glories and sufferings, can never be anything but an inspiration for our future. If we make it an idol to be worshipped instead of an inspiration, we jeopardize our future and betray those past generations we claim to celebrate and respect.

The robustness of a culture or a civilization is dictated by its attitude towards the past. Should we be slaves to the past or should we study the past for lessons and inspirations that will enable us to build a better future? As Jews we are obliged to respect our forefathers but not obligated to emulate them. As President John Kennedy once said: "the past has a voice, not a veto".

The Jewish people, especially, must cultivate futurist habits of thought, such as the ability to envisage desirable and possible alternative futures. Asking the right questions about current developments and cultivating the ability to recognize opportunities in unexpected events are essential attributes of rational policy making, which is a pre-requisite to a *meaningful* existence.

Creative thinking about the future differs from long-term planning. A planner in the United States, for example, would discern demographic trends and suggest building more retirement homes for an aging Jewish community. A futurist would explore the implications of the Jews being the oldest ethnic group in the United States and consider questions such as: how might this affect Jewish political influence over the coming decades? How might it affect support for Israel? What might it mean – culturally, psychologically, and spiritually – when Israel becomes the largest Jewish community in the world?

What will be the political status of world Jewry when the Moslem population of the United States surpasses the Jewish population and becomes increasingly organized and wealthier?

There was no need of futurist thinking until the Industrial Revolution. Before that, what we learned from our grandparents we could teach to our great-grandchildren and know it would have relevance for their lives. The aim of education was to pass the values and culture of past generations onto future generations, a kind of benevolent dictatorship of the past over every aspect of our lives. But after the Industrial Revolution the rate of change increased greatly and since World War II even more so. Changes no longer occur over several lifetimes. Radical changes occur constantly, every day of our lives. Individuals living today experience more change in one year than whole generations experienced only several hundred years ago. What we thought we knew several years ago we are not so sure we know today. How can we educate our children when we have to constantly reeducate ourselves?

To optimally exploit the historic opportunity the "flat world" is offering us we must first answer questions such as: how might the technology that is creating this new global order affect the social, economic, political, spiritual, and Zionist development of Israel and the Jewish people? What opportunities does this present to Israel and the Jewish people?

THE FUTURE BELONGS TO THE INDIVIDUAL

If we don't recognize the essential individualism of young Israelis (Jew *and* non-Jew) and Diaspora Jews we will be unable to construct a social, economic, and Zionist policy that rationally addresses the problems, challenges, and opportunities of modern Jewry and Israeli democracy. We require a new Zionist ideology that accommodates the radical individualism of globalization and the Internet.

The term Jewish *people* is meaningless unless it has significance for the Jewish *person*. If we do not recognize that the individual is a finite, one-time entity compelled to fill his or her life with meaning, then growing numbers of young Jews may see no reason to cultivate Jewish aspirations. The 21st century search for social solidarity and community is real and palpable. But in my view it is essentially different from the communalist ambitions of 19th and 20th century idealists in that it is primarily a pre-requisite for individualistic self actualization and not a call for idealistic self abnegation. It may be that a renewal of the original kibbutz ideal (not a misplaced loyalty to outmoded kibbutz frameworks) will have a serious role to play in this new reality.

In the 21st century *the individual is king*. As much as this statement might offend the social ideals of 20th century "progressives" it is nonetheless a simple fact of life. If we are to build a just society, with the necessary solidarity required to live a civilized life, we must accept the centrality of the individual as axiomatic. Denying or denigrating individualism will not lead to greater social justice or solidarity – it will only hinder it.

I am not endorsing individualism as an ideology. I am claiming that the rapid rate of change demands it. Centralized management or management by committee (even democratically elected committees) is no longer appropriate. Management has to be decentralized as decisions must be made in real time and cannot wait for decisions from above. This requires the empowerment of the individual. Modern technology – encapsulated in everything connected to the Internet – empowers the individual like no other previous technology. Individual bloggers, to mention just one example, have had as much impact on our politics in recent years as major media outlets. Just ask Dan Rather.

The notion that *Every Individual (is) a King* was an integral part of the social and political thought of Ze'ev Vladimir Jabotinsky, the founder, ideologue and political leader of Revisionist Zionism (the chief opponent of David Ben Gurion's Labor Movement). For him this was a fundamental value. Given the requirements and characteristics of our globalized world, this abstract value has now become a concrete practical necessity: economically, sociologically and psychologically. This is as true for Diaspora Jews as it is for Israelis. The aspirations, ambitions and dreams of a young modern Jew from Tel Aviv, a kibbutz or a development town are not different from those of a young modern Jew from New York, London, or Paris. Even the younger generation of Israel's non-Jewish minorities has begun to develop the same aspirations and ambitions as their Jewish counterparts.

By what standards should we evaluate the relationship of the individual to the community? I believe in the following way.

The **Individual**: Classical Zionism focused on the Jewish *person* as much as the Jewish *people*. Zionism saw the uplifting of the Jewish person and his or her individual *self realization (Hagshama Atzmit)* as the means by which the Jews could be renewed as a people.

The **Community**: Human beings are social animals. We cannot fulfill our individual potential and give meaning to our lives in isolation. What kind of communal frameworks do we need to realize our potential? The kibbutz was supposed to have provided the answer to this question. But it pursued an unsubstantiated "ideal" of human nature instead of asking what practical tools actual kibbutzniks needed to realize their individual potential. It is doubtful whether Israel could have been created without the heroic collective contribution of the kibbutz. Yet since its heroic period ended, it has had difficulty in reinventing itself as an agent of *individual* self realization in line with its own original ideology.

The **Economy**: We require an economy that enables us to realize our individual potential. It has to be innovative and profitable, providing ever-increasing options that reflect the possibilities of the new global reality. An inefficient unproductive economy hostile to the new global reality will not suffice.

The **Society**: What kind of society can sustain the kind of economy we need without selling ourselves to economic considerations only?

This is a challenge facing all humanity but Israel, supported by World Jewry, could take a lead in addressing it. Our bold utopian social history, tempered by practical experience, provides us with moral and intellectual resources unavailable to other societies. The vast reserves of social idealism within American and European Jewry would be able to find a creative outlet in contributing to such an ambition. That they would be doing this within a Jewish framework would constitute a major barrier to assimilation.

The **Country**: What kind of country do we need? We need a Jewish country: demographically, socially, culturally, politically, and even economically. We need a country in which the modern Jew can realize his or her ambitions as part of the new global reality and not sacrifice individual ambitions to those ideologies which place us in opposition to the world reality now being created.

The **World**: What kind of world do we need and how will Israel's economy, society, culture and country relate to it? No country or nation dwells alone. It never has, does not now and, given the new global reality, certainly never will. Indeed, world developments of the past 200 years have probably influenced Jewish history more than other nation's.

HISTORICAL ANALOGY

The Jews have already had to deal with a similar revolutionary period in the Industrial Revolution. It would be useful to review the impact this period had on us. The three most important events of the past 200 years of Jewish history have been: the creation of the state of Israel, the creation of North American Jewry and the Holocaust. All three would have been inconceivable without the means of production and transportation provided by the Industrial Revolution.

The first Zionist Congress, which took place in 1897 in Basle Switzerland, could not have taken place one hundred years earlier on anywhere near the same scale or format. Hundreds of Jews from all corners of the earth came to Basle at a specified time and took part in a discussion pertinent to the future of the Jewish people. Up until the 19th century and the Industrial Revolution such a mass convocation would have been impossible.

In 1797 no railroads and steamships existed and consequently no mass movement of people and no large hotels. There were no mass-distributed newspapers (as there were no technical means to produce them or literate market to consume them) and no reliable international mail or telegraph system. The organizational existence of the Zionist movement depended on the Industrial Revolution and so, too, the physical existence of the Zionist enterprise in the Land of Israel.

Opponents of Zionism often used the argument that Zionism was unrealistic because a wasteland could not absorb millions of Jews. Zionists replied that this may have been true in the past but the technical and engineering skills and the scientific knowledge of the Industrial Revolution would enable us to turn this wasteland into a flourishing garden productive enough to absorb all the Jews who wished to come. This argument has been confirmed by history.

Between 1870 and 1914 an estimated thirty million people immigrated to the United States to work in new American industries. This mass immigration was possible because of the new transportation technologies of steamships and railroads. Two million Jews were included in this migration. From a minor Jewish community during the Civil War, American Jewry had become, by World War I, one of the largest and certainly the most powerful and influential community in the Jewish World. The rise of Nazism and its industrial methods of murder made North American Jewry the largest Jewish community in the world by the end of World War II.

Democratic capitalism, the product of the Industrial Revolution, as well as its precondition, made American Jewry the richest, freest, most powerful and self-confident Jewish community in history. American Jewry's power mobilized wisely was one of the preconditions for the creation of the State of Israel, an event that altered Jewish history and further increased the self-confidence of Jews as American citizens.

Industrialization, and the secular Enlightenment values and scientific frame of mind that had made it possible, created new concepts of human civilization and interaction that stimulated German Jewry to create the Reform, Conservative, and neo-Orthodox versions of Judaism – the modern Judaism familiar to us.

As we have seen, the advent of industrial civilization was a revolutionary event in Jewish history. When considering the Internet Revolution we should be aware of even more opportunities and far-reaching changes awaiting the Jews in the 21st century.

THE ENLIGHTENMENT AND THE JEWS

Even before the Industrial Revolution the Jews were profoundly affected by other universal developments. Foremost amongst these was the European Enlightenment. Zionism itself was a late product of the secular humanist Enlightenment and had no problem conforming to its moral standards. Zionist leaders from Herzl, to Jabotinsky to Ben Gurion propounded Enlightenment values.

There are also inherent parallels between Enlightenment scientist Francis Bacon's maxim that it was humanity's task to penetrate Nature and tear her secrets from her and the Zionist imperative to conquer the wasteland. Adam Smith and Karl Marx – both products of the Enlightenment – hoped that their endeavors would result in a new man: more rational, just, and moral. This ambition is reflected in the Zionist aim to create a new type of Jew: more independent, less obsequious and more heroic. Without the Enlightenment concept of the *New Man*, it would have been impossible to develop the Zionist concept of the *New Jew*.

Modern Jewish life is inconceivable without the Enlightenment and the development of science and capitalism. Science and commerce were the basis of the modern humanist revolution as well as the prerequisites for eventual Jewish emancipation. Science and commerce are ethnically neutral, and reward competency and imagination regardless of the religious or cultural affiliation of those exemplifying them. Together, they were the basis of a major paradigm shift. Countries that took part in this shift prospered, those that rejected it became backward.

It is no accident that Holland, the first commercial republic, possessed a built-in resistance to ethnic discrimination and that Spanish and Portuguese Jews found refuge there from the Inquisition. Renaissance humanism, the Scientific and Commercial Revolutions it engendered, and the European Enlightenment that encapsulated these developments were the prerequisites to Jewish emancipation and the birth of modern Judaism and the modern Jew.

The Enlightenment/Industrial Revolution paradigm has been responsible for the greatest material and moral progress in human history. Its technological promise has stimulated a great advance in our moral, ethical, and even spiritual expectations. Few of us would be willing to return to a period when 70% of children died before the age of five or to live without electricity and modern medicine.

THE INTERNET REVOLUTION

The Internet Revolution parallels and perhaps even exceeds the revolutionary impact of the industrial revolution and constitutes the new human environment the Jews must deal with. The advent of the Internet represents a radical change in the intellectual and spiritual environment of the human race. It provides us with an entirely new framework in which to pursue humanity's cultural evolution. It enables human beings to create and innovate in distinctly new ways. Rabbi Jonathan Sacks, chief rabbi of the United Hebrew Congregations of the British Commonwealth has noted:

> The Internet is one of the most wondrous developments of all time...From...earliest days...(until) the West caught up with the idea, Judaism was predicated on universal education and the democratic access to knowledge. Knowledge, said Francis Bacon, is power. That is why, through most of history, it has been jealously guarded by elites. Judaism is not a religion of elites; least of all in the arena of knowledge...the Torah is the heritage of every Jew. We all have a share. We are all expected to learn. We each have a right to know. Today, because of the Internet, the vast treasury of Jewish knowledge is open to everyone...what the Web allows us to do is to share the thoughts of teachers throughout the world and sense the fact that we are a truly global people, linked by the shared act of learning.

This emerging historical force requires the radical transformation of the centralized institutions and organizations that have developed since the Industrial Revolution. We must develop new methods of human and Jewish organization and governance to be in tune with the experiences and expectations of the Internet generation.

CONCLUSION

A new paradigm of society is being born, based on new developments in science and in the organizational possibilities of industrial, scientific, and technological civilization. This is the world we live in. These are the practical, spiritual, and moral challenges we must deal with. The Jewish people must develop a cultural paradigm that relates to this world in constructive ways particular to itself.

What can we take from the cultural resources of the Jewish tradition that will enable us to creatively confront this reality and provide spiritual added value to the modern Jew in the 21st century? The answer to this question is the key to a flourishing and meaningful Jewish way of life.

This book is an attempt to answer this question. It is divided into two parts. Part I presents a condensed but comprehensive picture of where the Jewish People are in 2007. Part II depicts an "imagineered" (and very optimistic) Jewish future from the vantage point of the year 2020. This is a device borrowed from Edward Bellamy's famous 19th century social fiction *Looking Backward from 2,000 to 1887* as well as from Theodore Herzl's futurist tract, *Old New Land*. It is a device that enables me to demonstrate a logical progression based on real organizations, real people and reasonable policy aims. Most of all, it enables me to forestall the accusation that I am dealing in fantasy. Critics of my imagineered future will have to cite errors in fact or mistakes in logic in order to confound my optimistic vision. There is of course no guarantee that my vision will be realized. This is a question of national leadership and will. But as Herzl said: "if you will it, it is not a dream"!

| CHAPTER 1 |

THE TRIUMPH OF ZIONISM

I t seems to me self-evident that a serious reevaluation of Jewish life must begin with the extraordinary success of the Zionist project in the 20th century. Israel, for better or worse, has dominated the Jewish landscape for as long as any of us can remember. Its successes and failures have stood at the center of Jewish discourse for over a half a century.

The aims of classical Zionism were to create a Jewish state, concentrate a majority of the Jewish People within that state, integrate peacefully into the Middle East, achieve relative economic independence and build a model society. Let's review the record.

- We have established a state which, despite Arab hostility, has become part of the world community.
- Israel is now the largest Jewish community in the world and within 10-15 years will be larger than the entire Diaspora
- We have created a vital and highly developed economy despite what some researchers estimate as 44 billion dollars of economic harm caused by the Arab boycott since the establishment of Israel.
- Israel has been slowly integrating into the region over the past two and a half decades (despite intifadas and wars).
- The model society is still a distant vision to say the least.

POLITICAL ACHIEVEMENTS

The last three decades have seen extraordinary political achievements that were but fantastic dreams during the first decades of Israel's existence. I would make the case that Sadat's visit to Jerusalem and the peace agreement with Egypt, the Madrid conference and the much maligned Oslo agreements with the Palestinians, as well as the subsequent peace agreement with Jordan represent Zionism's greatest triumph since the creation of the State of Israel.

I say this because there has been an essential asymmetry between Arab and Zionist strategy following the creation of the State. Zionist strategy strove for Israel's peaceful integration into the region while Arab strategy strove to drive the Jews out of the region. *The peace process, as flawed as it is, is an unstated Arab admission that their strategy has failed and that Zionism's has succeeded.* This will remain the case no matter what the fate of the peace process following the second Intifada, the second Lebanese War or any other future crisis. What has been done cannot be undone, no matter how hard radical Islamists and Arab nationalists (and some Jews) try. They cannot deny that they sat with us in the same room, negotiated and signed peace treaties with us, conducted economic activity with us and made their own initiatives regarding a comprehensive settlement. Nor can they reverse other consequences of these developments, such as Israel's improved relationship with the rising powers of China and India which had been hindered because of these countries' identification with the Arab cause. Even something as extreme as Egypt and Jordan revoking their treaties with Israel would not and could not cause China and India to revert to a position of *status quo ante* regarding their relationship with Israel.

ECONOMIC ACHIEVEMENTS: BECOMING SILICON WADI

These political developments have had direct positive consequences for Israel's economic health. Israel is a small country and dependent on exports. From 1991 (the Madrid Conference) to 2000 (the outbreak of the second Intifada) 60% of the growth in Israel's exports were to countries with which we did not have full diplomatic and economic relations before 1991 (such as China and India). This was a major factor in Israel's overall economic growth which averaged 4-5% a year during this period. Israel's economy grew by 40% in the 90's and we became a world class high-tech center – Silicon Wadi. This enabled us to absorb over one million new immigrants (which along with natural increase grew the Jewish population of Israel by 25%). This is why *the peace process, no matter how flawed, is a Zionist asset in and of itself.*

As a consequence of these economic achievements Israel has ceased to be dependent on Jewish philanthropy and will soon achieve independence from American aid. This is an outstanding accomplishment given the challenges facing Israel. Many Diaspora Jews as well as non-Jews are under the mistaken impression that Israel would still not be able to survive without American aid or Diaspora contributions. The truth is that funds raised for Israel by all Jewish organizations represent about 1% of Israel's GNP and 2% of Israel's budget while American aid represents about 2% of Israel's GNP and 4% of its budget.

In 2006 only 120 million dollars of American aid was for civilian purposes. It was the last year Israel received civilian aid. In contrast, before the election of Hamas the United States had been giving the Palestinian Authority 350 million dollars a year. All American aid to Israel is now military and totals a little over 2 billion dollars a year.

This is much less than the 40-50 billion dollars a year the American military spent to defend Persian Gulf countries between the two Iraq wars.

The military aid provided by the United States to the Moslem Gulf States totaled over a half a trillion dollars between the two Iraq wars. The military aid given to Israel during the same period was between 25-30 billion dollars. The difference is how both are itemized in the American budget. Israel's is listed as foreign aid, while aid to the Gulf States' is reflected in America's military budget. This is also the case for America's NATO contribution. It is not listed as foreign military aid to Europe, nor is the money that tens of thousands of American troops pour into the local economies of these countries listed as foreign aid.

What is not commonly known is that most of America's military aid never comes to Israel and has no economic impact on the local economy (unlike the economic impact of the American troop presence in Europe and in the Persian Gulf). 75% of American military aid to Israel is deposited in American banks and used to buy American military supplies (generating jobs for an estimated 50,000 American families).

25% of the military aid is discretionary and comes directly to Israel. This is usually used to finance research and development of arms systems – such as the Arrow anti-missile missile – that Israel can do more efficiently than the United States (with subsequent savings to the American taxpayer). Israel is also a major provider of much of America's human intelligence about the Middle East. The military relationship is much less one-sided than generally perceived and of minor importance to Israel's *economic* wellbeing.

The threat to stop military aid as a means to pressure Israel into making decisions it would not otherwise make is simply wrongheaded. Fortunately this is recognized by most sophisticated policy makers in the United States and Europe. They know that Israel could now manage its security without such aid but also know that any arbitrary moves would make Israel more stubborn, not more flexible. They also know that a possible reaction might be to make its implicit nuclear capability explicit. This would almost certainly limit room for diplomatic maneuver and inflame the area even more.

Compared to the trillions of dollars of indirect military aid given to Europe and Japan during the Cold War (and even now) by way of the stationing of hundreds of thousands of American troops and powerful naval fleets, American aid to Israel is a bargain – especially as it is the only military aid America gives to any of its allies that does not entail the stationing of American troops.

The declining impact of the Arab boycott; the opening of formerly closed world markets; the legitimization of Israel as an object of international investment and the continued growth of the Israeli economy will more than make up for the end of Jewish and American aid. Ending the false sense of security American aid gives Israel might even compel organizational and administrative efficiencies that would be beneficial to the Israeli economy in the long run. The point is that Israel has succeeded in becoming an independent country, a triumph of human energy, will and perseverance.

THE SUCCESS OF THE ZIONIST ANALYSIS

Classical Zionism claimed that European civilization could not sustain vibrant Jewish communities in modern times. Anti-Semitism and the appeals of assimilation would eventually erode and destroy the possibility of Jewish existence in Europe. Naive faith in modern universalistic solutions to the Jewish problem such as liberalism or socialism was a delusion. The success of these ideologies would lead to increased assimilation, while their failure would lead to mass disappointment and social frustration. This would result in virulent anti-Semitism.

The above prediction unfortunately has been validated. Progressive ideologies alone have not been able to eliminate European anti-Semitism and its eventual expression in social and political behavior. One could be a liberal or socialist anti-Semite even as one spoke of universal brotherhood.

"Progressive" Europeans claimed that the Jews could achieve social and political liberation if they ceased to be Jews and became members of the general human community. Many Jews, anxious to please "enlightened" opinion, attempted to become the mythological "cosmopolitan" human being. That strange cultural mutation, the cosmopolitan Jew, with a pathological desire to be free of his Jewishness, was born. "Jew, Jew, Jew," cried Portnoy in Phillip Roth's *Portnoy's Complaint*. "Why can't I just be a human being?"

On the other hand, 19th century European *Liberal Nationalism* claimed that there is no such thing as a general human community. There are rather a myriad of national, ethnic, and religious communities interacting with one another to their mutual benefit. The true progressive aim, therefore, should not be to deny our cultural differences but to create frameworks in which interactions between different human communities could be positive and creative. The great 19th century Italian liberal nationalist Mazzini was one of the clearest spokesmen of this view and he had a tremendous impact on Zionist thinking. Moses Hess's seminal *Rome and Jerusalem* (1862) – demonstrating how ancient peoples like the Italians and the Jews could reconstruct themselves and make a universal contribution to the entire human race – was a reflection of Mazzini's thinking. Jabotinsky's national-social agenda was similar to Mazzini's thinking.

Today we might use the environmental paradigm to re-enforce Mazzini's insights. Environmentalism recognizes that "mono-culturalism" (the cultivation of a single crop over extensive areas) endangers the health of the entire ecological system. Ecological systems that have an increasing variety of species and ever-increasing interactions between these species are healthy, vigorous, and robust. Ecological systems that have a diminishing variety of species and diminishing interaction between these species are sick and susceptible to collapse. Each species preserving its own identity and integrity in dynamic interaction with other species enhances the essential robustness of the entire ecological system. What is true of natural culture is also true of human culture.

A vigorous society would be characterized by an ever-increasing number of subcultures contributing their particular outlook and creativity. Nations and ethnic groups that strive to preserve their integrity and identity in *respectful* interaction with the rest of humanity enhance the essential robustness of all human civilization. A homogenization of human culture into a cosmopolitan monoculture would impoverish the human spirit to the point of endangering the very prospects of human survival. This view constitutes the ideological validation of Zionism as well as other liberal nationalisms in the 21st century.

Hess's *Rome and Jerusalem* anticipated this ecological analogy by predicting the universal contributions a renascent Italian state and a renascent Jewish state would make to universal human civilization, not as their primary rationale, but as a natural consequence of performing the tasks necessary to reconstitute themselves.

Has Hess's thesis stood the test of time? Have the necessary tasks of the Zionist enterprise contributed to universal human civilization? Examples are numerous. Following are only two:

- The Zionist success in reviving the Hebrew language (one of the greatest achievements of Zionism) has become a 'light unto many nations'. The Welsh, Scots, Irish, Dutch and others are all using the *Ulpan* system to renew their languages or teach them to new immigrants.

• The Zionist success in creating a modern society in an arid ecology has also been a 'light unto many nations'. Israeli foresters have been asked to oversee and advise massive arid zone reforestation projects in countries as diverse as Mexico and China. Israeli water engineers and agronomists advise developing *and developed* countries all over the world.

Such universal contributions have been a natural consequence of Israel fulfilling its national needs and not because of a desire to be universalistic humanitarians.

The Enlightenment call to the Jews to join the general human community was really a call for Jewish assimilation and the end of the Jews as a people. Particular collective Jewish existence was thus de-legitimized by the ideologies of modernism (see Hertzberg's *The French Enlightenment and the Jews*, Jewish Publication Society, 1968). This was but a short step to de-legitimizing the very physical existence of the Jews. The *Final Solution* of the Nazis could be seen as a perverted stepchild of this simplistic universalistic impulse.

ANTI-SEMITISM, JEWISH SELF-HATE AND ZIONISM

The pathology of Jewish self-hate, whereby Jews themselves agreed to their own de-legitimization, was born out of this universalistic view. No one could be more contemptuous, sarcastic, and venomous against any expression of Jewishness (religious or Zionist) than the cosmopolitan Jew striving to be part of Gentile society.

Unfortunately for them, cosmopolitan Jews were also attacked by anti-Semites because they were cosmopolitan and so without authentic cultural roots. *Rootless cosmopolitan* became a synonym for Jew in Stalinist literature and was often a prelude to anti-Semitic activity.

The cosmopolitan Jews did not blame their "progressive" attackers who embraced universalistic ideologies of brotherhood – how could they be anti-Semitic? Instead they blamed the Jews. They blamed Eastern European Jews who refused to give up their particular Jewish behavior and mannerism. They would ask "how can the Gentiles be expected to accept us as part of their community if we remain separate?" They also blamed Zionism which generated questions of dual loyalty by embracing "reactionary" and "anachronistic" positions of nationalism. They would ask "how can we expect the Gentiles to accept us as loyal and patriotic citizens if we fight for a separate Jewish State and how can we expect progressives to accept us if we become reactionary nationalists?"

The Jews were attacked *because* they wanted to remain separate communities, *because* they presumed to national sovereignty and *because* they dared assume they could assimilate and be true Germans or true Frenchmen. East European Jews were resented because they spoke poor German and French with a terrible accent, and cosmopolitan Jews were resented because they spoke perfect German and French, often better than "authentic" Germans and French. Today Russian Jews are resented either because they presume to be true Russians or because they choose to remain Jews. Germany could not tolerate the Jews, nor could Poland, Rumania, Hungary, or the Ukraine. Vast areas of Europe have or will soon become empty of Jews. The Zionist analysis has proven accurate for most of Europe.

SELF-EMANCIPATION

European cultures, unlike the mosaic of American culture, are normative. They have a national language, national customs, and national music and literature. For romantic nationalists, these are natural organic products of the internal developments of their particular people. Outsiders can imitate or pretend to be a part of these cultures, but they can never truly be part of them.

In the view of modern anti-Semitism, which is largely a perverted outgrowth of modern romantic nationalism, the very attempt to pretend to be part of the authentic nation by "inferior" ethnic groups infected the national culture and spiritual health of the nation. Accommodating this pretense was in their minds a disease that caused the authentic nation to be "sick". It had to be expunged. The extreme expression of this sentiment led to the Nazis.

All of this was quite clear to early Zionist thinkers. In 1882 Leon Pinsker, a Russian Jewish supporter of the Enlightenment and assimilation, rethought his position after a pogrom and wrote his profound tract *Auto-Emancipation.*

Analyzing current events and anticipating some of the above dilemmas, he concluded that the only solution to the Jewish problem was to be found within the Jewish will to self-emancipation, that is, the Jews taking ultimate responsibility for their own future. He argued that putting one's faith in universalistic ideologies to solve the Jewish problem is a self-deception and would result in even greater suffering.

He wrote that the Jews must take responsibility for their own fate and cease to base their future on the modernist fiction of human progress and the eventual perfection of humankind. As we have seen in the 20th century (the bloodiest in history) human progress is no guarantee for producing better human beings, it is only a guarantee for increasing human power.

The message of Zionism was that we cannot depend on liberals or socialists to emancipate us. We must arise and emancipate ourselves. If we wish to earn the goodwill of the Gentiles we must do so in the old-fashioned way – through power. We must become political and create power that would enable us to defend ourselves. In the era of nationalism and the nation-state, this meant Jewish nationalism and Jewish statehood as a means to Jewish self-emancipation.

Following Pinsker, Theodore Herzl, another assimilated Jew who had no knowledge of the *Auto-Emancipation* essay, came to the same conclusion. In response to the famous Dreyfus affair (1894) he wrote *The Jewish State* (1896). This work was less intellectual than *Auto-Emancipation* but was written in a more compelling and popular style that was more accessible to the Jewish masses and so had greater impact.

Although the Zionist analysis was preoccupied with European Jews most Zionists believed it was also relevant for Jews in the Moslem world. They believed that the inevitable rise of nationalism in the Moslem world, in response to European nationalism, would exacerbate the inherent precariousness of Jewish existence in the Islamic Diaspora, until viable Jewish communities could no longer sustain themselves in the Moslem world either.

America, on the other hand, was recognized as different from the outset. Leaders such as Ben Gurion and Jabotinsky realized that a different kind of Jewish community was being created. Yet in the final analysis most Zionists believed that sooner or later viable Jewish communities would also be difficult to sustain in America. The reasons might differ from those in Europe and the Islamic world, but in the end Jewish viability would also erode in America. The conclusion was that Jewish survival in the modern era (the era of industrialism, liberalism, capitalism nationalism, socialism, and individualism) depended on creating and sustaining a modern, democratic Jewish State in the ancient Jewish homeland where, because of objective and subjective developments, the majority of Jews would eventually live.

NORMALITY AND ABNORMALITY

The question of Jewish normality has been a preoccupation of Zionism since its inception. Early Zionists claimed that Jewish existence without Jewish sovereignty in a Jewish homeland was abnormal and dangerous. Since the Holocaust, the need for a Jewish State has become an almost universally accepted norm of world Jewry, with only a few exceptions. The only caveat being that most Jews (presumably including most Israelis) do not now believe that the entire Jewish people must settle in Israel.

Classical Zionists saw the dispersion not only as a physical exile from the Land of Israel, but also a spiritual exile from a Jew's authentic self. Zionists viewed exile as the primary cause of a perceived distorted economic structure of Jewish society. Exile was also responsible for creating a peculiar kind of Jewish personality and mode of behavior: insecure, fearful, self-conscious, hyper-energetic, over-compensating.

Exilic Jews were thus characterized by a unique combination of self-loathing and self-love that exiled them from their genuine selves. Some Zionists even went so far as to claim that this collective socioeconomic abnormality combined with the behavioral abnormality of so many Jews made the Gentiles uncomfortable and contributed to anti-Semitism. For them, Zionism would not only cure the Jews of their abnormality, it would also cure the Gentiles of their anti-Semitism.

Exile and cure are recurring themes in Zionist literature. Exile was the disease; return to the homeland was the cure. Today, however, Israelis in contact with Diaspora Jewry would probably agree that Jews in the West are not living an abnormal existence in exile. Yet many reflective Zionists would still argue that while the classic Zionist analysis might leave a lot to be desired in its particulars, its basic ideological assumptions have stood the test of time.

THE SUCCESS OF THE ZIONIST ANALYSIS

What is the historical record of this Zionist analysis? In the Islamic world, millennia-old Jewish communities have all but disappeared. The only viable Jewish community in the Middle East is Israel. "Progressive" opinion would blame Zionism and Israel for this development. "Progressives" would claim that the Jews always lived well under Moslem rule; that Islam only *appeared* to become anti-Jewish because of the unjustified provocations of Zionism (unjustified because Jewish nationalism itself is unjustified). In truth, the Jews always lived under the sufferance of the Moslems. Jews were always a protected *People of the Book* as long as they agreed to their inferior position and, like the Blacks in the American South, 'kept their place'. A good antidote to the politically correct romanticism of the wonderful relations between Jew and Arab during the golden age of Islam would be to remember that the great medieval Rabbi Maimonides (the Rambam) fled Spain not because of Christian persecution but because of the invasion of a fanatic Moslem sect.

The modern Islamic rejection of Zionism sprang from the Jewish pretension to equality. For Moslems it was intolerable that an inferior people presumed to assert their national and hence their human rights alongside of Islam and create a sovereign state within which even Moslems were bound by laws passed by a Jewish majority. Jews as individuals can be tolerated, but Judaism and Jewish aspirations cannot be treated as having equal value. Blaming Zionists for anti-Jewish violence in the Middle East and elsewhere is akin to blaming American Blacks for anti-Black violence because they dared to assert their rights and refused to accept the role designated for them by others.

The Zionist prediction about what would happen to the Jews of Europe was unfortunately vindicated in the 20th century. The Nazis almost physically exterminated European Jewry. The Communists almost spiritually exterminated Soviet Jewry. European Jewry's population dropped from about 9 million before the war to about 3 million after the war, and to about 2 million at the fall of Communism. Hundreds of thousands have disappeared through assimilation in the Soviet Union. British Jewry has declined from a community of well over 400,000 in the 1960s to under 300,000 today, due mostly to assimilation and emigration. The 600,000-strong French community suffers from mass intermarriage.

Since the fall of Communism, well over a million Jews have emigrated from the Soviet Union. With less than 1 million Jews and fewer births than deaths and thousands emigrating every year, the future of Russian Jewry appears bleak.

As Zionism has predicted, physical and spiritual persecution has combined with tolerance induced assimilation to spell the end of European Jewry. Within the next several decades – little more than a century since Herzl and Pinsker – fewer than one million Jews will live in Europe and fewer than one hundred thousand in the Moslem world, less than one-tenth the population of a century ago.

The Zionist claim that the exile cannot sustain viable Jewish communities in modern times appears vindicated. There is, however, a powerful argument for one major exception to the Zionist case: *American Jewry*.

| CHAPTER 2 |

THE SPECIAL CASE
OF AMERICAN JEWRY

I agree with those who claim that America is different and American Jewry is different. This difference is why American Jews are often indifferent to fundamental Zionist arguments and are not impressed with Israeli intellectuals and politicians preaching the classic Zionist message. The reason is that unlike 19th century European Jewry, Zionist arguments have had little significance for the 20th century American Jewish experience. The American Zionism of Brandeis and Kallen has been and still is a more accurate reflection of the American Jewish experience. Their argument was that the creation of Israel would imbue American Jews with more self-confidence and self-esteem and would thus make them better *American* citizens. Looking at the status of Jews in American society before and after the creation of the State of Israel one would be hard put to deny the validity of their position.

What is so singular about America that makes it less amenable to the classic Zionist message? At the most fundamental level it is because America's history, cultural origins and foundational mythologies are different from those of Europe. The United States is the only Western country whose mythologies are Old Testament and not pagan. The Bible and biblical metaphor form the foundation of American culture, not the Greco/Roman, Teutonic or Druidic myths which reflect the pagan roots of European culture.

Exodus and the search for the Promised Land is the dominant American metaphor. America has transformed the idea of the Promised Land into an amorphous concept called *The American Dream*. The Exodus metaphor appears in various degrees in all five of the foundational cultures of the United States:

- the Puritan forefathers
- African Americans
- the saga of the West
- the immigrant saga
- suburbia

THE PURITAN FOREFATHERS

The metaphor of the Pilgrims and Puritans was Hebrew. England was their Egypt and the King their Pharaoh. The Atlantic Ocean was their Red Sea and America the New Canaan. Some historians even claim that the Jewish holiday of *Succoth* inspired Thanksgiving. Both are harvest holidays commemorating God-inspired and God-guided deliverance in the wilderness. America's Puritan heritage and other fundamental Protestant influences have engraved the American character with the Hebrew imprint. American mythology is Old Testament. Neither Thor nor Jupiter lies at the bottom of the American character, but Moses, the Chosen People, the Promised Land, and redemption. The Puritans saw their religion as a continuation of the Covenant of Israel but under a different administration.

One message of the Old Testament was that a nation as well as an individual could be in covenant with God. They intended to establish such a nation, doing God's work, on the shores of the *New Canaan of America*. This vision still has enormous impact on the American character today and partially explains that sense of exceptionality that

Americans have about themselves (which so often infuriates other nations).

Many of these early Americans found justification for their distaste for absolutism and divine right in the Old Testament. They believed that government must be moral before it is political. The equal protection clause of the Constitution has its roots in the belief that all men are equal in the eyes of God.

The infatuation of the Jews with America equals that of the Protestant Americans with the Hebrew heritage. Early Sephardic Jews, in an attempt to identify America with the Promised Land, asserted that the American Indians were descendants of the Ten Lost Tribes. Ashkenazi Jews called America the *Goldene Medine* – the golden country (the land of milk and honey). The word *America* has quickened the hearts of Jews for years, in ways that may be surpassed only by the word *Israel*.

Revolutionary America and modern Israel are also strikingly similar. They are the only countries in the world to be established in whole as a country, a society, and a culture, by a group of founding fathers inspired by visions of a universal role. It is the messianic prophetic message that informs both experiences, for better and for worse.

AFRICAN AMERICANS

The second foundational culture is that of the African Americans. It is also based on the Exodus metaphor, although in both negative and positive ways. It is both an escape from the Egypt of America and a journey to the promised land of America. The Black spirituals, rooted as they are in the slave experience, sing of deliverance from slavery, going into the Promised Land (*Go Down Moses*), and crossing the river Jordan (the Mississippi serving as a substitute – how water-deprived Israelis wish it were so!).

Examine the speeches of Martin Luther King and other Black civil rights leaders and see how often the Exodus and redemption metaphors repeat themselves. In King's last speech before he was murdered, he likened himself to Moses, and I paraphrase: "I may not enter the Promised Land with you; I may only stand on the mountain top and look in, but you will enter."

Even though African Americans constitute only 15% of the population, Black culture has made a disproportionate contribution to American culture. What, after all, is American music? Jazz, rock and roll, blues. This music can be traced back to Black church music, founded on biblical mythology and metaphor.

THE SAGA OF THE WEST

The great migration to and conquest of the West is another great Exodus. The West with all that it represents (cowboys, individualism, and freedom) is still a fundamental saga of American culture. These pioneers were looking for their own promised land. They wanted to leave the perceived injustices of the East for freedom, dignity, and happiness.

The Great Plains were the Sinai desert. Read the correspondence and the diaries of these pioneers and you will discover redemptive biblical language in its full force. James Michener's popular novel *Centennial* captures the sense of destiny of these pioneers. Prayers of guidance and of thanksgiving were their daily lot. The phrase *Manifest Destiny* connotes a God-given right and task, similar to the God-given right and duty of the Hebrews to conquer the Promised Land.

American politicians spoke about the God-given rights of the God-fearing nation to these lands. Native Americans were sometimes seen as hostile Canaanites who had to be eliminated to make room for God's people. To justify their elimination the white settlers often called them *Amalek*.

THE IMMIGRANT SAGA

The immigrant saga is the fourth foundation of American culture. America was the Promised Land for a mixed multitude of downtrodden peoples looking to escape the persecutions of modern day pharaohs and find freedom and dignity. Their Exodus was in steerage, not on camel or donkey, and the ocean, as with the Pilgrims, was their Sinai wilderness. Their sighting the Statue of Liberty at the gateway to the Promised Land after their travails remind one of the Israelites looking over the Jordan River from Mount Nebo into their Promised Land after forty years in the desert.

SUBURBIA

The foundation cultures of the Puritans, African-Americans, the West, and mass immigration are all variations of the Exodus metaphor. In addition, we have the materialistic redemption dream of suburbia, a caricature of the Exodus metaphor, but no less powerful than the other foundation cultures in molding the American persona.

Fleeing the imperfect city – looking for the American Dream of perfect happiness and harmony in the promised land of new perfectly designed communities. The promised land American Dream of suburbia has resulted in a peculiarly idiosyncratic American literary form called suburban angst, based on the failure to find perfection and harmony, something that only Americans would even seek. Some claim that the elusiveness of this American Dream has had crucial formative impact on the American psyche, culture, and polity. How un-French, how un-German, how un-Italian - how Jewish! Is this one reason that so many Europeans feel foreign in American culture while so many Israelis feel at home?

AMERICAN CULTURE AND PATRIOTISM

Europeans often deride the United States for having no culture. This is both true and untrue. The United States certainly has culture and profound cultural creativity. But unlike Europe, America has no generally agreed upon normative culture. It is a mosaic of subcultures. American cultural life has no center and no periphery. Neither Jews nor anyone else can be accused of not assimilating like the Eastern European Jews in Germany, or assimilating too much like Stalin's 'rootless cosmopolitans' in the Soviet Union. Can anything be more amenable for Jews than this?

Patriotism in the United States is also different. It is not measured by swearing loyalty to Volk, Fatherland, or hereditary sovereign; it is measured by swearing to uphold and defend the Constitution. Civil rules of behavior, not race, blood, or mythical appeals to the land and historical legend determine what a true American is. One does not pledge allegiance to the tribe; one pledges allegiance to the flag and the republic for which it stands: that is, to the Constitution, which is the republic. A true American is one who adheres to Americanism, to the American way of life, not to particular bloodlines. This is why Chinese, Blacks, and Jews can talk about 'our Pilgrim forefathers' without a sense of absurdity.

Objective Challenges

Is it any wonder then that few other ethnic groups in the United States have surpassed the Jews in believing in or taking advantage of and fulfilling the American Dream? Judged by the practical standards of Americanism, the Jews are the most American of all the American ethnic groups. They are the wealthiest, best educated, most professional, most organized ethnic group in the United States. They have a higher percentage of political representatives in proportion to their size than other minorities – even representing areas that have no sizable Jewish vote.

So why, with all this, is Jewish existence in the United States still a matter of doubt over the next fifty or sixty years? The organized American Jewish community has significant pretensions in regards to Jewish history. It has developed the two-center theory of modern Jewish existence in opposition to the one-center theory of Zionism. American Jews would agree that classical Zionism is right in regard to the rest of the Jewish world but wrong in regard to the United States. The rest of the Jewish world may be "in exile" but American Jews are not. They might put it thus: "We are obviously not in our ancient homeland, but we are still at home".

They would claim that the American Jewish relationship to Israel is similar to that of Babylonian Jewry during the Talmudic period and the formation of Rabbinic Jewry. They would claim that modern Jewish life can and will survive in at least two more or less equal centers: Israel and North America.

The many positive developments within American Jewry of the past twenty years are often cited by the proponents of the two-center theory as proof of the vigor of the American Jewish community. But these developments must be examined in light of more basic negative trends; trends documented and commented upon in great detail by the American Jewish community itself.

Demographics, for one, are a major concern. For although the Jews have always been a small people and although size itself is not a prerequisite to cultural success, continued existence is first of all biological and numerical. Below a certain critical mass, even small peoples have difficulty sustaining communal identity and cultural creativity. In this regard, the long-term statistical trends are not promising. The American Jewish Committee's Yearbook has reported that American Jewry is shrinking by about ½% a year (in contrast to Israel's Jewish community, which is growing by around 1 ½% a year before *aliya*).

Other indicators show that this rate of shrinkage is likely to increase. By the end of the first decade of the 21st century, 50% of all marriages involving Jews may be intermarriages. Although some of these intermarriages result in the couple rearing their children as Jews, most at present do not.

In addition, the Jews are the most elderly ethnic group in the United States. Some reports claim that the median age of the Jewish community is already over 45 (as compared to about 35 for the general American community and 25 for Black and Hispanic Americans). The median age of American Jewry is, therefore, already beyond the age of reproduction.

Moreover, various social factors – such as a higher proportion of feminist consciousness – lead Jews of reproductive age to marry later than other ethnic groups. The biological future of the American Jewish community, therefore, is not bright *if present trends continue*.

One reason why this has not been more dramatically felt is the large influx of Israeli, Russian, and Latin American Jews into the United States over the last three decades of the 20th century. It is significant that even with this influx, demographic erosion continues as documented by American Jewish organizations themselves.

THE FUTURE OF AMERICAN JEWRY

According to some demographic research, Israel has already become the world's largest Jewish community. What cultural, psychological, and spiritual repercussions will this have for both communities? This question has yet to be addressed. Within the first two to three decades of the 21st century, more Jews will be living in Israel than in all Diaspora communities combined.

As the largest, wealthiest, most powerful Diaspora Jewish community in the world, American Jewry must redefine itself and play a special role in the creation of a new Judaism and a new Zionism. Its special character, unique potential and vital position within the American republic make its contribution to the Jewish future indispensable. It is a partner that the Jewish people must have in order to fulfill its potential.

America's democratic principles, scientific knowledge, and technological power make it the natural spiritual and practical partner of the Jewish people. America's heritage seems to have predestined her to become the primary supporter and partner of a renascent Jewish people and the State of Israel.

American Jewry must create a coherent "ideology" of what defines American Jewishness. This must be an American, not an inherited European or Asian ideology. This could be an updated expression of America's Hebraic roots and could offer a coherent framework that enables American Jews to combine being world, American, and Jewish citizens. American Jewish educators might conclude that teaching about America's Hebraic roots in Hebrew school outweighs running bar mitzvah "factories". Teaching children to declaim prayers they do not understand has certainly not proven effective in preserving or enhancing Jewish identity.

Schizophrenia is the natural condition of today's thinking American Jews. Fascinated with and enthusiastic about America,

American Jews have always struggled to relate to America and their Jewishness at the same time and with integrity. They are often uneasy Americans and uneasy Jews. The 2000 Democratic vice presidential candidacy of Joseph Lieberman, while of great historical importance, failed to ease this angst in a meaningful way.

American Jewry must confront what it means to be Jewish in modern, secular, 21st century, pluralistic America. Nostalgic *yiddishkeit* can no longer suffice, as more and more Jews move further away from the East European tradition.

A real American Jewry must be created – with its own values and an agenda sometimes in tension with Israel – for the sake of Jewish cultural flourishing in general and for the sake of Israel. A mature 21st century Zionism would advocate as one of its central tenets "the reconstruction of the American Diaspora" while discontinuing the use of barren slogans pertaining to the "negation of the Diaspora".

| CHAPTER 3 |

REINVENTING ZIONISM

I am neither a classical Zionist nor a post-Zionist. I suppose I might call myself a neo-Zionist. I accept the fundamental premise of classical Zionism that Jewish sovereignty over a small area of the earth's surface is a prerequisite to physical survival and a necessity for Jewish self esteem and self confidence. In this sense I am an updated version of American Zionism even though I have made Israel my home for the past 40 years. I am always amused when I meet proponents of classical Zionism dwelling in the Diaspora while I, an American Zionist, live in Israel. This curiosity reenforces a belief that has become axiomatic with me. Modern individuals choose to live where they find the greatest potential for their own self-actualization – whether material, intellectual or spiritual. It is the living individual person and his or her needs and desires that dictates reality, not the abstract principles of some ideology.

FROM JEWISH PEOPLE TO JEWISH PERSON

Classical Zionism dealt with the physical and cultural survival of the Jewish people. Neo-Zionism must concern itself with the *Jewish* survival of the individual Jewish person. The ideology, policy and strategy of Zionism in the 21st century must be to provide a framework for the optimal self-actualization of the individual Jew. It must deal with the concrete social, economic and psychological reality of the modern, university trained non-orthodox Jew instead of abstract historical and philosophical concepts of "*the* Jewish people".

There is no one objectively definable "*the* Jewish people". There are, however, many real individual Jewish persons. There is no objectively definable "*the* Jewish Problem". There are millions of individual Jewish problems. The preoccupation with the optimal self-actualization of the Jewish person is the precondition for the physical and cultural success of the Jewish people.

Preoccupation with *self*-sacrifice, literally the sacrifice of the individual *self* as a precondition for Zionist "idealism" is a prescription for the end of the Zionist Project. This assertion reflects the essential social and Jewish differences between the 19th century and the 21st century. It is a difference that can best be understood by referring to Abraham Maslow's famous pyramidal hierarchy of human needs:

- *Biological and phsiological needs*: air, food, drink, shelter, warmth, sex, sleep, etc.
- *Safety needs*: protection from elements, security, order, law, limits, stability, etc.
- *Belongingness and love needs*: work group, family, affection, relationships, etc.
- *Esteem needs*: self-esteem, achievement, mastery, independence, status, dominance, prestige, managerial responsibility, etc.
- *Self-actualization needs*: realizing personal potential, self-fulfillment, seeking personal growth and peak experiences.

Maslow's insights enable coherent explanations of various cultural and sociological phenomena. They explain the "generation gap" of the 60's when the well-off children of depression-bred parents rebelled against their parents' preoccupation with the lowest two levels of Maslow's pyramid and created a culture dedicated to "finding themselves". They also explain why hundreds of thousands of third world and former Soviet bloc guest workers find Israel such a desirable place to work, live and raise their children while so few North American and European Jews even consider it.

Israel enables the guest workers to satisfy Maslow's first level: food, clothing etc. In regards to the second level, physical safety, Israel is still more physically safe than the countries they come from. It is also often a more desirable country in which to raise and educate their children.

Present day Israel is problematic for most Diaspora Jews – *especially* those that attempt aliya. Many western immigrants live in an existential dissonance. They made aliya as part of a larger search for self-actualization which entailed a degree of idealization of Israel. Their motive for moving to Israel was the search for Maslow's highest level. Yet the harsh reality of Israel often forced them to revert to preoccupation with Maslow's two lowest levels. Hence the dissonance.

This same dissonance is spreading amongst growing numbers of well-educated young Israelis. They are becoming increasingly tired of Israel's chronic security and economic problems. This phenomenon manifests itself in several ways. It appears to be mostly limited to the non-Orthodox. The self-actualization of Orthodox Jews is inherent in their religious belief. The self-actualization of non-Orthodox Jews is contingent on the economic, educational, social and cultural opportunities provided by the society they live in.

Because of all this it is generally agreed that Zionism is in crisis. The crisis expresses itself in post-Zionism in Israel and a steady decline of identification of young Diaspora Jews with Israel. When the modern Jew, Diaspora or Israeli asks: "does classical Zionism resonate with meaning for me and for the challenges I must face?" the answer is most often a resounding NO.

Some Zionists would dismiss the very question as self-indulgent individualism, reflecting decadence, a loss of values and a decline of commitment to Jewish survival. But does decadence cause the question to be asked or is decadence a result of the question not being answered? Can an ideology truly address the problems of a collective unless it is meaningful for the individuals who constitute that collective? The lack of a positive answer constitutes the emotional foundation of post-Zionism.

HISTORICAL BACKGROUND

Zionism developed on the background of 19th century European civilization in response to the unique conditions of 19th century European Jewry. It drew inspiration from the 2,000-year-old desire to return to Zion but was not synonymous with that desire. It was a 19th century political development and is inadequate to the needs of the 21st century for the following reasons.

• half of Israel's Jewish population are of non-European origin,
• two-thirds of the Diaspora lives outside Europe,
• 20% of Israel's total population is not Jewish (and not European).
• we no longer live in the 19th century.

These compelling facts necessitate a far-reaching reinterpretation of Zionist ideology.

19th century Europe was characterized by the Industrial Revolution and the rise of capitalism, liberalism, nationalism and socialism. These developments released forces that made the situation of the Jews increasingly intolerable but also supplied the means by which they could liberate themselves. Opponents of Zionism asserted that a wasteland could not absorb millions of Jews. Zionists responded that using the new industrial means of production the land could be redeemed, converting it from a wasteland into a garden. In this way the modern industrial reality became both a concrete instrument and a propaganda tool of the Zionist enterprise.

The progenitors of Modern Hebrew language and literature (Bialik and Ben-Yehuda) were part of a universal European historical phenomenon called cultural nationalism. When they appeared, many European nations were already modernizing their language and literature, transforming them into useful tools for their modern national aspirations. The Jews had a longer road to take, considering that Hebrew of any sort was not their daily spoken language, but the project itself was not as unique as we suppose.

Every political party within the Zionist Movement – and since 1948 within the State of Israel – has been rooted in the 19th century European political reality. 19th century 'isms', such as liberalism and socialism, provided Zionism with the raw material to construct its political culture. Dependence on 19th century 'isms' is characteristic of the entire world's political culture, but the Jews feel its negative consequences more because of their particular character and their greater need to adapt to the 21st century environment in order to endure and flourish.

The environment of 19th century Jewry was characterized by the lack of a state, abysmal poverty and the lack of basic human rights. More than 80% of world Jewry lived under tyrannical or authoritarian regimes and Jewish life was characterized by what socialist Zionism called an abnormal socioeconomic structure, the so-called inverted pyramid. This concept suggested that "normal" nations possess a pyramidal social and economic structure, with most of the population in industrial and agricultural production, a minority in services, and an even smaller minority in intellectual and spiritual endeavors.

THE PREOCCUPATION WITH NORMALITY

The word normal derives from norm, that which is standard. 19th century Jewry was a reverse image of the period's economic norm.

Unlike their Gentile neighbors only a tiny number of Jews were in agriculture; a slightly larger number were in industry and the majority made their living from services and intellectual pursuits. The consequences of this *abnormality*, according to classical Labor Zionists, were unhealthy social, cultural and psychological characteristics that contributed considerably to anti-Semitism. After all, why shouldn't presumably normal peoples be troubled by the presence of an *abnormal* people living in their midst?

One of the main tenets of Labor Zionism was that the Jews had to cure themselves of their abnormality through the catharsis of physical work. The creation of Jewish working and peasant classes became not only a political, economic and social necessity but increasingly became of spiritual, almost religious, value in and of itself. Out of this was born the myth of the *halutz* or the pioneer. The early pioneers of what are known as the 2nd and 3rd *aliyot* (immigrant waves) saw themselves as national, social, cultural and spiritual pioneers. This tiny band produced many of the great leaders of the pre-state entity as well as the early leaders of the state. They included David Ben-Gurion, Levi Eshkol, Berl Katzenelson, Pinhas Sapir and Golda Meir.

During this historical phase, the Zionist project was self-evident: to create a Jewish State which, by guaranteeing the civil rights of the Jews, would release their productive energies and allow the creation of a Jewish working and peasant class. This would solve the problems of abject poverty and the supposedly abnormal socioeconomic and psychological-cultural structure of the Jewish people.

Zionism had tremendous impact on the masses of East European Jewry because its analysis and its program resonated with meaning for their lives as individuals living in a particular historical context.

THE PARADOX OF SUCCESS

Classical Zionism's primary purpose was to substitute normality for the abnormality of an exilic existence. It succeeded, and this success is the root of our dilemma. We now have a Jewish State in existence for nearly 60 years. This fact alone completely changes the character of Jewish existence, not only for the Jews who reside in the state but also for Jews the world over. It is impossible to understand the psychology, organizational structure and behavior of Diaspora Jewry today other than in the light of Israel's existence. Statehood, not statelessness, is the dominant Jewish fact and the major operating principle behind any analysis of Diaspora Jewry.

Consequently, pre-state Zionist polemics are meaningless for the everyday concerns of the modern Jew, including the modern Israeli Jew. The fact that the educational content and the organizational structure of much of Zionist life still relies on this outmoded paradigm reflects what is wrong with current Jewish life in Israel, in the Diaspora and in regard to Israel-Diaspora relations.

Classical Zionism claimed that the creation of the state would fundamentally alter the character of Diaspora Jewry. They would be prouder, more independent, more autonomous and more self-confident. This has happened, yet Zionist functionaries have not come to terms with it, because it implies the normalization of Diaspora Jews and contradicts their conviction that Diaspora life is inherently abnormal.

A vacuum has been created. The space filled by a story book version of Zionism, which few take seriously, is one cause of the current superficiality of Jewish life. Zionism's biggest problem is that it has realized its aims and its self-appointed spokesmen have not formulated an up-to-date message that resonates with meaning for modern Diaspora and Israeli Jewry. Zionism is an example of the principle that nothing fails like success. The state exists and Jews are normal, now what? This situation has given birth to a detrimental phenomenon called post-Zionism.

The axioms of Zionism are being called into question even by people who still identify as Zionists. Do the Jews really require a state of their own to guarantee their civil rights? The vast majority of Diaspora Jews now lives in the Free World and possesses more civil rights as individuals than the citizens of Israel. They have more religious freedom than Israeli Jews, are free from the various impositions of the Orthodox rabbinate and they have the freedom to choose any trend of Judaism without fear of discrimination. No censor limits their freedom of speech and they are unhindered by the need to do military reserve duty.

Is the Jewish State a prerequisite to ending Jewish poverty? The vast majority of 21st century Diaspora Jews are not poor. Diaspora Jews usually have higher per capita incomes than other ethnic groups in their respective communities *and* also higher than Israel's.

In addition the inverted pyramid has become the norm for the entire developed world. Since World War II, developed societies around the world have been in a process of inverting the pyramid. In the United States, less than 2% of the work force is in agriculture, less than 15% in manufacture and the rest in services or information exchange. What was once considered abnormal has become the standard by which all modern societies judge themselves. In this sense, the social and economic structure of much of the developed world has become *Judaized*. In retrospect, the inverted pyramid was not an abnormality but actually a precursor to what Alvin Toffler called Third Wave civilization (in his book of the same name).The First Wave referred to agricultural society, the Second Wave to industrial society and the Third Wave to the post-industrial services civilization we live in.

THIRD WAVE ZIONISM

Zionism's purpose was to solve the problems of living Jewish persons and enable them to enjoy and realize their human being without sacrificing their Jewish being and to realize their Jewish being without sacrificing their human being. This can be the only justification for the existence of Israel and Zionism, and if Israel does not do this then what is its *raison d'etre?*

Many young Diaspora and Israeli Jews have grown distant from Israel in recent years because Zionism is a 19th century ideology trying to come to terms with a 21st century reality. Using Alvin Toffler's metaphor of the three waves I believe that it is a second-wave instrument trying to answer the problems of a people who, as individuals, are at the forefront of creating a third-wave civilization. This outdated model of Zionism finds it difficult to provide solutions for a growing list of modern Jewish problems. Survey what is wrong with modern Israel and in many cases you will find an underlying Zionist position that ceased to be relevant decades ago. Preoccupation with outdated questions of classical Zionism is depriving many Israeli and Diaspora Jews of the historical space needed to actualize themselves as individuals. Zionism aimed at easing the integration of the Jewish people into modern life. This would enable the individual Jew to realize himself or herself as a modern human being without having to sacrifice Jewish identity. This was to be done in a way that would create specifically Jewish frameworks that give Jewish identity an added value to the individual's ambitions to actualize his or her capacities.

Such an ambition requires a stress on the future. From Herzl to Ben Gurion, Zionism has been preoccupied with the future and not with the past. Ben Gurion's desire that Israel be a *light unto the nations* for both moral and practical reasons sprang from his concern for the future of Jewish existence. The moral and the practical were inextricably linked in his mind. He and many of his contemporaries were repelled by Zionists who moralized in the abstract instead of finding practical solutions.

IDEOLOGY, THEOLOGY AND IDEALS

Zionism is an ideology not a religion. It is not a belief system, but an intellectual tool for analyzing the situation of the Jewish People. It is also a program for improving that situation. Ideological conclusions pertaining to a given situation at a certain point in history do not necessarily pertain to a different situation at a different point in history. Nothing is more foolish, therefore, than to continue to endorse a certain program because it worked in the past. A course of behavior that worked in a past radically different from the present is almost guaranteed to fail in the future. Ideologies are based on ideals, but *ideology* and *idealism* are not synonymous. Some ideals such as brotherhood, equality, justice, freedom and liberty are positive. One may be liberal, socialist, conservative, or religious and embrace various interpretations of these ideals. Honest people embracing radically different ideologies can sustain civilized cooperation with mutual respect when their basic ideals are the same. This constitutes the very foundation of democratic society. But ideals and idealism can be negative. Adolph Hitler, the Ayatollah Khomeini, the Kamikazes and the Red Guards were also idealists.

This is why when, in the context of the current Israeli political debate, we hear the phrase "at least they are idealists," we should want to know what ideals we are talking about before we become enamored. If the ideals in question reflect explicit or implicit racism, contempt for judicial due process and democratic procedure or equality before the law, we should not be impressed.

When this kind of idealism is framed by a belief system that presumes to know the will of God vis-à-vis current political questions and is thus capable of morally justifying every kind of outrageous behavior, it is time to draw a line and say: *we are no longer one*. The ultimate product of such "idealism" was Yigal Amir – the murderer of Yitzhak Rabin. Dogmatic loyalty to old ideas, organizations and ways of doing things is not proof of the purity of one's Zionist credentials. It is proof of stupidity and is guaranteed to bring failure.

ZIONISM IN THE 21ST CENTURY

Zionism for the 21st century must undertake to accomplish the following:

- mobilize and direct the energies of the Jewish People into practical and creative activity as intense as the pre and early state eras,
- transform Israel into a society with the highest possible scientific, cultural and social standards,
- turn Israel into an economic super power with one of the highest per capita standards of living in the world,
- enlist the abilities of the entire Jewish People to create new frameworks and services geared to answering vital world needs in the 21st century,

Israel must become the tool of Jewish civilization not its aim. Jews do not exist for Israel, Israel exists for the Jews. The recent decision by the Israeli government to invest hundreds of millions of dollars dedicated to making Israel the premier world power in water technology is an encouraging sign in the right direction.

Such a national vision, if expanded into other areas, would:
- excite the imaginations of our young people,

- provide them with concrete frameworks in which to exercise their idealism,
- necessitate solving many social problems now plaguing Israel.

Our national visions ought to evolve into national-universal visions with obligations for a national-universal people. Unless we develop a new paradigm of Jewish existence we will fail to develop the instruments necessary for *particular* Jewish existence in the 21st century. Israel cannot truly become a Jewish center unless it becomes a world center and cannot become a world center unless it becomes a Jewish center. At present Israel is often perceived to be part of the problem not part of the solution. Becoming part of the solution would strengthen Israel's international position and world Jewry in general.

The small nation-state is becoming an economically irrelevant concept even as ethnic and cultural nationalism increases throughout the world. Economically, Israel is not even a country. Its GNP is equivalent to a medium-sized city in the developed world. The concept of the sovereign nation-state is being supplanted by a profusion of *transnational nation-states* interacting with one another in a growing complexity of human activity.

Transnational nation-states would be capable of preserving the cultural integrity of ethnic groups or nations while facilitating their economic and political integration into the new transnational reality. Integration into the new transnational reality is becoming essential to the preservation of the national and cultural sovereignty of small peoples. A transnational Zionism is required for the 21st century; a Zionism that reflects the transnational character of the Jewish people and, increasingly, the human race.

FROM PIONEERING OUTPOST
TO GLOBAL METROPOLE

A transnational Zionism would recognize that Israel's population is smaller than greater Boston or greater Philadelphia. It would understand that an entity the size of medium-sized cities and isolated from its immediate geographic surroundings cannot pretend to copy Japan or the United States or even Korea and Taiwan.

I believe that Israel's models should be Boston and San Francisco. We are in competition with them for the hearts of the modern Jew. They, not Damascus or Teheran are Zionism's greatest survival challenge. This being so, we must transform our self-perception from pioneering outpost to global metropole providing services to the entire world, thus reflecting the aspirations and utilizing the skills of a "world people" (*Am Olam* as it is called in Jewish tradition).

An estimated quarter million university students reside in greater Boston and generate billions of dollars of economic activity. Boston's other major economic activities include health services and science-based industries as well as other related services. Boston serves not only Massachusetts and New England but the continental United States and the world. It is not a regional city but a world city, a metropolitan node within the planetary communications and services system.

Israel can become such a metropolitan node. Israel's multicultural, multilingual human resources enable it to surpass other metropolitan nodes in many areas. The model of Boston should be a *light unto the Jews*. Modeling itself on Boston turns Israel's disadvantages into advantages and makes it a more suitable instrument to serve the needs and aspirations of the modern Jew.

When Israel properly understands and exploits modern telecommunications it can become a world-class supplier of educational, engineering, health, legal, financial and other non-tangible services. These services would enable the growth of new science-based industries as well as the absorption of many communications and medical personnel, scientists, lawyers, engineers, and educators – professions the Jewish people prefer.

FROM TALKING THEORY TO SOLVING PROBLEMS

Could the Boston analogy help us solve many of the problems facing Israel and world Jewry? Let us engage in a mind experiment and see.

POPULATION INCREASE AND IMMIGRANT ABSORPTION

Israel has had trouble absorbing its own native born children, as well as skilled *aliya* in the rewarding and interesting occupations they desire. By constructing a society, culture and economy based on the inadequate paradigm of the Second Wave nation-state, we have created frameworks and policies that are dysfunctional to our national interests.

Transforming Israel into a world metropole serving the needs of the world economy would create a chronic shortage of academically trained personnel and raise the standard of living. The advent of Israel as *Silicon Wadi* is a sign that Israel has already begun this process. And notwithstanding the periodic crises of the so-called New Economy, it is evident that Israel's future lies in this direction.

JEWISH WORK AND FOREIGN WORKERS

Moralizing about Jewish unwillingness to work has assumed the dimensions of a national sport. This judgment, however, is drawn from an image of work left over from the classical Zionist myth of the inverted pyramid and the need to create a new Jewish class of peasants and proletarians. In truth, Jews have traditionally been allergic to poorly paid, boring work and are not impressed by Tolstoyan ideologues singing the praises of physical work which supposedly raises the spiritual level of the individual. They know that boring, by any other name, is still boring.

On the other hand, those connected with Israel's knowledge-based economy know that well-paid, interesting employment often produces a work ethic higher than the Japanese or the Americans. Unfortunately we have inherited a "pioneering" economy unsuitable to the temperament, aspirations and skills of the Third Wave Jewish people.

Economic development depends as much on temperament and cultural characteristics as on economic theory. The Japanese succeeded because they built an economy which reflected the relative strengths and the mentality of the Japanese people. We must build a Jewish economy which reflects the relative strengths and mentality of the Jewish People.

ISRAEL-DIASPORA RELATIONS

Israel-Diaspora relations have been based on self-righteous Israelis preaching about immigration, or Diaspora Jews giving money to or lobbying on behalf of Israel. The relationship is still primarily based upon Diaspora philanthropy and political activity on behalf of Israel. In recent years both the percentage and the absolute number of people contributing to Israeli causes have dropped. More contributors are looking for different kinds of Jewish causes to support and the real value of the Diaspora's yearly contribution to Israel has greatly declined. Significant investments in Israel can involve only a small percentage of the community and therefore cannot constitute an alternative model to contributions.

In addition to fundraising and investments, we should be developing a United Jewish Appeal of human resources enabling educators, scientists, engineers, artists, media personnel, and managers to contribute their skills and not only their money. The conditions that would enable us to absorb unlimited immigrants and Israelis would also enable us to exploit the talents and energies of many professional Diaspora Jews in meaningful activity centered on national-universal projects.

The revolution in transportation, telecommunication and information exchange enables us to redesign our concepts of Zionism and Israel-Diaspora relations. Air travel time from New York to Los Angeles is 6 hours and New York to Tel Aviv 10 hours – a difference of only four hours. Moreover modern communications enable instantaneous contact. Thousands of American Jews move from coast to coast every year. Given the proper conditions why couldn't they also move to Israel?

This model of Israel-Diaspora relations can assist in the fight against assimilation by investing our practical and educational endeavors with new future-oriented content. This will stimulate Jewish ambitions by exciting idealism and satisfying self-interest within Jewish contexts. An Israel that becomes a *light unto the nations* is capable of doing that.

THE SOCIAL-ETHNIC GAP

Only a Third Wave society is capable of erasing the disgrace and danger of Israel's social gap. Social solidarity is not only an ideal. It is a practical necessity for a healthy society. Israel's social gap is a greater danger to the success of the Zionist enterprise than the Arab armies.

We require tremendous resources to close this gap. We cannot generate such resources from a Second Wave economic base; just as we cannot close the income gap on the basis of what industries in competition with India, Pakistan, and the Philippines can possibly pay.

Those who might boast about Israel's past success in creating a "real" Jewish working class should note that most of those workers were Oriental Jews who did not want to be workers. They certainly did not want their children to be workers and resented the Ashkenazi ideologues who praised physical work that they themselves would not think of educating their own children to do.

Not only is the existence of a Jewish working class in Israel not part of the solution to the Jewish problem, as early Zionism required, it is now a major part of Israel's social problem. Conventional industry in competition with cheap-labor countries creates a strong vested interest in keeping educational and social levels low to create cheap pools of labor. This perpetuates the gap.

More than one million Israeli workers earn less than $750 a month. The existence of a Jewish working class in the 21st century has resulted in a Jewish serf class. Knowledge-based enterprises, on the other hand, have a strong vested interest in raising educational and social levels to create a talented labor pool. It is time that Zionism undertook a conscious rejection of the inverted pyramid myth.

JEWISH-ARAB RELATIONS

The strategy of enlightened Zionism was and must continue to be to integrate peacefully into the region. Our relations with the Arab countries, the Palestinians and Israeli Arabs cannot, however, rely on such empty concepts as trust, goodwill or the brotherhood of all men. They must reflect our own long-term interests rooted in a foundation of power. Power and enlightened self-interest, not holding hands and singing "we shall overcome," must underlie our relationship with the Arab world and the world at large. Only a Third Wave Zionism, based upon the concept of Israel as a world metropole, can provide the requisite power to confront the Arabs as we move into the 21st century.

None of the above is Pollyanna-like fantasy. It is within our capabilities to accomplish all of it. The only question is, do we as a people have the will?

| CHAPTER 4 |

REINVENTING ISRAEL-
DIASPORA RELATIONS

I believe that in order to rejuvenate Zionism we have to reinvent Israel-Diaspora relations. The driving force behind a revitalized Israeli-Diaspora relationship should be the Diaspora and not Israel. The Diaspora should take a greater responsibility for addressing the challenges of creating an enhanced Jewish future and cease being satisfied with being subordinate to Israel's needs. I say this as an Israeli and as a Zionist and claim that this would be best for Israel and Zionism.

This approach would replace the present character of Israel-Diaspora relations in which Diaspora resources are directed to the social problems of Israel as a supplemental force in education, welfare and immigrant absorption. A renewed relationship should be concerned as much with Diaspora needs, values and desires as with the needs of Israel.

We cannot ignore how Israel's problems affect Diaspora Jewry. The second Intifada had both psychological and security repercussions for many Diaspora communities and triggered a new wave of anti-Semitism in Europe. It is simply immoral for us Israelis to claim that the Diaspora has no right to interfere in Israel's affairs when Israel's affairs have such an impact on the Diaspora. Or as Napoleon's Minister Talleyrand would have said: "Monsieur, it is worse than immoral, it is stupid"!

Since North American Jewry constitutes 80% of the Diaspora, it will often be the particular Diaspora performer in what follows. This in no way discounts the productive and perhaps even leading role European Jewry and other smaller Jewish communities might play.

TOWARD A NEW PARADIGM

The dominant Jewish paradigm since the creation of the state has been a highly efficient Diaspora fundraising apparatus transferring money to Israeli institutions dominated by Israel's political society. The sums have been diminishing in real terms in relation to Israel's GDP. This is a positive indication of Israel becoming a mature, developed economy and society. This would not have been possible without the Diaspora financial contribution.

The traditional Israel-Diaspora relationship was a tremendous historical success. But success breeds satisfaction with the forms, structures, values and subcultures that made it possible. Self-satisfaction breeds complacency which is a certain recipe for a breakdown of imagination and creativity.

The traditional financial relationship has had only modest effect on most of Israel's citizens for the past several decades. Some Israelis would even claim that Diaspora contributions have become dysfunctional to the healthy development of Israeli society. They would claim that these contributions are an indirect subsidy to the power of Israel's political society at the expense of the development of Israel's civil society. The time has come for a new paradigm wherein these relatively small sums go directly to Israel's civil society with the aim of improving Israel's quality of life. That is, to more efficient and effective public administration; innovative educational initiatives and national projects (such as energy independence) that could mobilize the energies and skills of large numbers of uninvolved Jews.

This would have great indirect impact on the economy. Efficiencies in public administration alone could save sums equivalent to the present Diaspora contribution, as would Israel achieving energy independence. The long term economic benefits of educational innovation are obvious. This is an approach familiar to investors – it is called leveraging. This would be a leveraging of Diaspora resources that would increase the effectiveness of Diaspora contributions and be of greater benefit to Israel.

A NEW RELATIONSHIP

Historically, the Diaspora has interacted with Israel primarily by way of Israel's political society, either directly with the Israeli government or indirectly by way of Israeli political representatives in the Jewish Agency. Israel's political society has also, in large part, mediated person-to-person and community-to-community projects such as *Project Renewal*. Reversing this order would create a more balanced and symmetrical relationship, since organized Diaspora Jewry is by definition a civil society.

The Diaspora interacted almost exclusively with Israel's political society because Israel did not have a dynamic civil society during its first decades. Today, however, Israel possesses a rich diversity of volunteer, self-help and citizen organizations that offer many opportunities for a wider, deeper and more mutually rewarding Israeli-Diaspora relationship.

Diaspora Jewry can take some credit for the development of this civil society. *Project Renewal, The New Israel Fund* and increased Federation emphasis on involving contributors in *specific* projects are some Diaspora initiatives that have helped nourish this civil society and have laid groundwork for the new relationship suggested here. The goal should be to deepen Diaspora contact with the rich tapestry of Israel's civil society which has reached a level of maturity whereby it can engage Diaspora Jewry's civil society as equals without the mediation of Israel's political establishment.

Diaspora Jewry needs to do this because Israel is the primary instrument by which the Jewish People interact with the world. Israel is the showcase through which the Gentiles perceive the Jews. Jews take pride in Israel's achievements in desert reclamation, its daring military exploits such as the Entebbe operation and the fact that other small, undeveloped countries often see Israel as a model to emulate. Even serious Palestinian intellectuals (off the record, of course) will tell you they see Israel as a model for their embryonic Palestinian State.

On the other hand, most Jews feel shame and dismay at Israel's mistakes. If Israel is Jewry's showcase and her actions affect all of world Jewry, the Diaspora has a moral obligation to "interfere" in Israel's affairs. Moreover, Diaspora Jewry does not require the approval of Israel's political establishment in order to cooperate with Israel's civil society in projects that affect all of world Jewry.

FROM FINANCIAL TO HUMAN RESOURCES CONTRIBUTIONS

Diaspora financial contributions were a necessary phase of Israel's history. In the pre-state era and early years of statehood these contributions produced astounding results. This approach, however, has now run its course. Not only is the Diaspora financial contribution of declining importance to Israel's economy and dysfunctional to the development of Israel's civil society, it has also become dysfunctional to Diaspora life – concentrating on the wealthy few to the detriment of more comprehensive community involvement. Many Diaspora Jews feel neglected by Jewish organizations and alienated from organized Jewish life because they do not have large sums to give and are thus marginalized or even ignored.

The emphasis should now shift from monetary contributions to Israel's political society to human skills contributions to Israel's civil society. This would be of greater benefit to Israel and would also enable Diaspora organizations to widen the base of Jewish involvement. It would attract individuals and groups presently disaffected with Jewish communal life. A chronic weakness of Diaspora life has been a lack of activities that interest significant numbers of Jewish professionals and academics and that could use their skills in meaningful communal activity.

The basic principle of this approach is to leverage declining Diaspora impact on Israel into increased impact on Jewish life in general. We could do this by creating coalitions around issues and projects that bear directly on Jewish welfare, have wide appeal for non-Jews and could involve large groups of heretofore unaffiliated Jews.

THE JEWISH ENERGY PROJECT

Energy is just such an issue. The greatest threats to the security of the Jewish People are Iran's nuclear bomb program, increased anti-Semitism and the growing radicalism of world Islam as well as large populations of hostile Moslems in Europe and North America. Financing *all* these threats are Persian Gulf oil revenues.

Iran could not finance its nuclear program if it did not have the export revenues of two and a half million barrels of oil a day. Saudi Arabia (whether its government or its citizens) could not spend billions of dollars a year in distributing anti-Semitic literature worldwide or financing Taliban style school systems throughout the Moslem world if it did not have the export revenues of eight million barrels of oil a day. Would Hezbollah and Hamas have achieved such organizational vigor without the support of Iran, Wahabi clerics and wealthy laymen from Saudi Arabia? The radicalization of European and American Islam is also underwritten by Persian Gulf oil revenues.

This dictates that the Jews formulate a coherent *Jewish Energy Policy* aimed at creating political alliances and economic instruments dedicated to downgrading oil as the dominant international commodity. Oil must once again become a commodity on a par with coffee, sugar and tea. (When was the last time the world was held hostage by the price of tea?)

Worldwide consumption of crude oil is projected to grow by 40% by the year 2020 if the consumption growth rate of the past several decades is sustained. Most of this supply increase will come from Persian Gulf countries. They have the largest proven reserves and these reserves are cheaper to develop than known and potential reserves elsewhere. Even if the real price of oil does not increase or even declines slightly, these militant anti-Jewish countries will benefit from a great increase in financial and hence political and military power. As a consequence, we may expect increasing support for terrorist organizations, anti-Semitic propaganda, and a heightened rate of development of non-conventional weapons of mass destruction.

A *Jewish Energy Project* would present Diaspora Jews with numerous opportunities to develop alliances with an assortment of pressure groups and economic entities thus widening the peripheries of positive Jewish influence. It would also give organized Jewish communities an opportunity to enlist uninvolved Jews interested in alternative energy and the environment.

Individual Jews, Jewish organizations and AIPAC should become active supporters of the *Set America Free Coalition* www.setamericafree.org. This organization brings together prominent individuals and non-profit organizations concerned with the security and economic implications of America's growing dependence on foreign oil. This coalition, organized by the Institute for the *Analysis of Global Security*, points out practical ways in which real progress toward energy security can be made over the next several years. Some Jewish individuals and organizations (such as the *American Jewish Committee* and the *Jewish Institute for National Security Affairs*) are already active with this organization. I suggest that support for this organization be equivalent to support for Israel. I say this as an Israeli because I realize that this is one of those keystone initiatives which, if properly leveraged, can effect revolutionary change. This would be to the benefit of Israel since what benefits the Jewish People benefits Israel.

Following are allies American Jewry might recruit around a project dedicated to making North America energy independent within the next 10 to 15 years, either as part of *Set America Free* or as the separate *Jewish Energy Project*:

Environmentalists: American Jews should support environmental organizations that push for alternative energy and conservation measures on federal, state, county and local levels.

Home Improvements Industry: American Jews should be active in trying to reduce per capita household energy consumption to the levels of Sweden or Germany. This means lobbying for tax write-offs for energy-saving home improvements and appliances. Allies would be industry and home improvement giants such as General Electric, Hewlett Packard, Westinghouse, Home Center, Home Depot, Lowe's and many more. These industries and their suppliers employ millions of people who might become better disposed to Jewish issues as a result of this initiative.

Organized Labor: The above policy would produce hundreds of thousands of well-paying domestic jobs and would appeal to organized labor. This could be a major factor in reestablishing organized Jewry's traditional alliance with organized labor.

Veterans and National Security Organizations: Energy is the primary strategic resource of the industrial world. Yet, for more than 30% of its energy needs and 50% of its petroleum needs, the industrial world depends on unstable countries such as Saudi Arabia, Kuwait, Venezuela, and Nigeria, or hostile countries such as Iran, Iraq, and Libya. This security lapse is causing great concern among veterans and national security organizations. They, too, are natural allies.

Educators: One might envision a *Twin Towers Energy Project* promoted throughout the school districts of the United States. Uniting the social studies and science departments, it would encourage school children to surf the Internet and engage in research to find low-cost energy conservation measures that they could install in their schools and at home. A system of *Twin Tower* clubs could be established and could piggyback on existing youth programs such as Boy Scouts, Girl Scouts and 4H. Children are by nature idealistic, and the combination of patriotism and environmentalism could galvanize them and create an irresistible grassroots movement. Such a project would enable Jewish teachers, a large and neglected segment of the community, to finally assume their rightful position in the Jewish community.

The two million Jews of Europe, including Russian Jewry, could promote their own version of a European energy independence project. European Jewry could help initiate a sister organization called

Set Europe Free. The South African, Australian, and Latin American communities could also pursue similar smaller scale initiatives.

Diaspora Jewry could leverage its limited power by building coalitions around projects of universal interest that also have direct benefit for the Jewish community and that could attract new groups of young Jews into active Jewish life. If this is done within the framework of Jewish values such as *Tikkun Olam* it could effect a spiritual regeneration, in addition to the political, economic and social benefits.

THE SPECIAL ROLE OF THE ISRAELI DIASPORA

The Israeli Diaspora, which may comprise as much as 15-20% of the North American Diaspora, should assume a special role in redefining Israel-Diaspora relations. Expatriate Israelis understand better than other Diaspora groups the needs and weaknesses of Israel. They are therefore less likely to be intimidated by possible protestations from Israel's political society regarding Diaspora initiatives.

The Israeli Diaspora has long been the stepchild of Jewish life, often looked upon askance by Diaspora Jews and condemned and boycotted by "official" Israel. In the eyes of official Israel, they are *yordim* – people who left Israel, as opposed to *olim* – people who immigrated to Israel. Emigration from and immigration to Israel is not just a sociological phenomenon as it is with other nations. Traditionally, it has had explosive moral implications. For official Israel, *yordim* were often pictured as traitors or as weaklings.

The attitude of native Diaspora Jewish communities toward these Israelis has been ambivalent at best:

- The fact that they had left Israel, often for good reasons, complicated communal and fundraising activities and confused

Diaspora emotions. Israel is idealized more by Diaspora Jews than by Israelis. The very existence of Israelis who left Israel challenged strongly held conceptions.

- The fact that they were Israeli in every way annoyed Diaspora Jews no less than the Israelis in Israel annoyed them.
- The *yordim* often did not participate in Jewish communal and institutional life. They often kept their distance and did not trouble to hide their condescension. For many Israelis, Diaspora Jewish life was a pale shadow compared to their Israeli experience. They did not camouflage this attitude and earned the resentment of many Diaspora Jews.
- Official Israel actively dissuaded the Diaspora communities from enlisting them. When they were enlisted, it was for practical reasons.

This approach to the Israeli Diaspora must undergo a far-reaching transformation. In the future, the Israeli Diaspora must become the bridge between Israeli and Diaspora civil society. They must become an ally of reformist forces in Israel. This is a role native Diaspora Jews have been loath to play and feel uncomfortable with.

The Israeli Diaspora must also assume a greater leadership role in the social and cultural life of the Diaspora community. For the non-Orthodox Jews especially, they are the most Jewish Jews. They offer a living model for a secular Jewish culture that is an alternative to Orthodoxy and an often shallow Diaspora Jewish life.

In effect, the Israeli Diaspora might fulfill the most Zionist pioneering function of the 21st century by assuming a leadership role in Israel-Diaspora relations. The law of unintended consequences may have turned the most maligned group in Jewish life into one of the most important players in the battle for an improved Jewish future.

| CHAPTER 5 |

REEVALUATING SETTLEMENT POLICY

Nothing has done more damage to Zionism and the situation of world Jewry than Israel's misconceived settlement policy. The direct and indirect impact that this has had on rational policy making has been disastrous. Since 1967 nothing has done more damage to Jewish unity and the status of Jews around the world. No rejuvenation of Zionism or reinvention of Israel-Diaspora relations can occur without a fundamental reevaluation of this settlement policy.

KIBBUTZ AND MOSHAV

During the pre-state and early post state era, kibbutz and moshav settlements epitomized Zionist strategy and activity. Their contribution was crucial in the struggle to create and sustain the Jewish State. They provided security in struggles with local Arabs as well as hostile Arab incursions from outside the Mandate area. They played a vital role in the absorption of Jewish immigrants and in creating Israeli agriculture.

Their heroic attempts to sustain equality of means as well as equality of opportunity invested the entire Zionist enterprise with a moral self-confidence that energized the Zionist pioneers and inspired world Jewry. It also earned the admiration of progressive non-Jews.

This had significant political benefits. Many liberal, socialist, and labor organizations around the world were in favor of the Zionist enterprise and the nascent Jewish State because of the kibbutz and other social experiments. Israel's standing with these organizations was a political asset second only to organized Jewry.

If you wanted to be an active Zionist during the pre-state and early state periods, you would become a member of a kibbutz or a moshav. By doing so, you would be contributing territorial, security, economic, moral, political, spiritual, and immigrant absorption value to the Zionist enterprise and the young Jewish State.

Mass Immigration Settlement Policy

Flaws in this settlement policy were perceived almost immediately after the creation of the State. The classic Zionist approach of filling up empty spaces with as many Jewish settlements as possible in order to guarantee Jewish ownership, contribute to security and determine borders, continued to be the backbone of immigrant absorption policy during the Jewish State's first two decades.

Hundreds of thousands of new Jewish immigrants, mostly from Africa and Asia, were directed to "Development Towns" in under populated peripheral areas. They were also directed to cooperative farming villages called immigrant moshavim. Cultural reasons ruled out the kibbutz as an option for this mass immigration.

Yet even in the early 1950s, some people active in the absorption process warned that this policy was an outmoded leftover from the pre-state era, unsuited to the needs of the newborn Jewish State. They noted that most of these immigrants came from technically backward societies and possessed few of the skills required to prosper in a modern technological society. It would be impossible to supply hundreds of small villages and dozens of small towns with the full menu of social, educational, and employment opportunities required. They predicted correctly that this settlement policy would perpetuate and deepen the social gap.

The critics claimed that the advent of the State, including an organized police force, border guard, army, and other requisite institutions, as well as recognized international borders, represented a fundamental transition from the pre-state Zionist project. The strategy of filling up every square kilometer with a Jewish population to prevent Arab squatting and the development of an Arab majority in certain regions such as the Galilee and the Negev were in their view anachronistic.

Instead of hundreds of tiny villages and dozens of small development towns, they suggested creating three or four major metropolitan areas. This would enable less per capita investment in infrastructure, as well as more efficient public services and employment opportunities for those people most in need. Some recommended developing Beersheba into a major city of one million inhabitants and Afula, Safed, and Tiberias into cities of a quarter million each. Such a policy would guarantee Jewish majorities in the Negev and the Galilee and better enable Israel to confront its inherited social gap.

Veteran leaders, who considered settlement activity the essence of what it meant to be a Zionist, dismissed these proposals. Rather than seeing settlement as a means, they viewed it as an end. They felt that its cessation would be a betrayal of a fundamental Zionist value. After the Six-Day War, the advocates of Jewish settlement in the newly conquered territories used this view to disarm and inhibit opposition.

THE CONSEQUENCES

The negative consequences of this policy are self-evident. The development towns and immigrant moshavim contain about half of the Jewish population under the poverty line. These settlements offer few opportunities for young people, many of whom move to the major cities, often to impoverished neighborhoods. Poverty and the social gap are thereby perpetuated into the third and fourth generations and the challenge of creating a Jewish majority in the Galilee and Negev is made more difficult.

The Arabs, on the other hand, have no predominately Arab city in which they would feel comfortable. Their traditional village environment, joined to the low status of Arab women both of which directly contribute to a low standard of living, resulted in a high birth rate. Consequently, more Arabs than Jews now live in these areas. This demographic dilemma has lead to an ugly phrase and an even uglier policy: *Judaizing the Galilee*. This refers to a proactive policy of trying to attract Jews to the Galilee by establishing numerous small Jewish hilltop communities.

The policy has "accomplished" several things. It gives us a feeling that we are really doing something about increasing the Jewish population of the Galilee – an illusion as the settlements seldom have more than several hundred residents. Their small size has compelled us to expend great sums of public money per capita on infrastructure. Establishing them requires the expropriation of land owned by Israeli Arabs – people who are citizens of the State. This has aggravated the alienation Israeli Arabs feel towards the State. *Land Day* is the yearly commemoration of and protest against the expropriation of Arab land for the benefit of Jewish development projects. The policy not only has not Judaized the Galilee but also has alienated and radicalized young Israeli Arabs.

This could have been avoided if we had concentrated on developing three or four major Jewish population centers in the Galilee. We could also have cultivated the establishment of a major Arab city of a quarter to half a million residents in the Galilee. The subsequent urbanization of the Arab population combined with a proactive affirmative action education policy for Arab women would have, by natural and enlightened means, greatly reduced Arab birthrates and the perceived Arab demographic threat. Moreover, such a policy would have eliminated the need for state expropriation of Arab owned land for Jewish projects and would have forestalled much bitterness and alienation of Israeli Arabs.

If we had pursued this alternative course we would have large and permanent Jewish majorities in both the Negev and the Galilee, the social gap would have diminished, and we would have a more positive engagement with our Arab citizens. Moreover, the moral self-confidence of many Israelis as Zionists would have been enhanced rather than eroded.

SETTLEMENTS IN OCCUPIED TERRITORIES

The settlement policies pursued in territories occupied in 1967 are an example of making a bad situation worse. The argument for or against the settlements in the occupied territories must be made based only on whether they are smart or stupid in regards to *what is good for the Jews*. In other words, what value do these settlements contribute to the Zionist project in the 21st century?

A good case could be made that some of the post-Six-Day-War suburbs of Jerusalem and the middle-class settlements contiguous to Israel's pre-Six-Day-War borders contribute to Israel's vital interests. The isolated ideological settlements, on the other hand, have been a tremendous burden. They have been detrimental economically and socially, as the vast funds poured into them could have been put to better use expanding educational services and building infrastructure. They have also consumed security resources that could have been better used elsewhere. The vast number of man-hours spent guarding settlements has undermined the army's training regime, something which became painfully apparent during Israel's recent incursion into Lebanon. They have also created a de facto border more than four times the length of Israel's border before the Six-Day War. Simple security calculus dictates that diminishing concentrations of soldiers on longer lines of defense equals less security, while higher concentrations of soldiers on shorter lines of defense equals more security. The recent disengagement from Gaza reflected this operational reasoning.

Almost every embarrassing political difficulty Israel has experienced since the Six-Day War has been because of these ideological settlements or their supporters, and not a single country in the world has changed its mind regarding the official, legally constituted borders of the State of Israel because of the settlements.

The settlements have also caused a great deal of alienation within many segments of Israeli society, tarnishing the label of Zionist, and weakening the spiritual fortitude and moral certainty of Israel at large. Many Israelis find the settlement subculture abhorrent and resent doing reserve duty because of it. By identifying Zionism with the settlements and calling the opponents of settlements post-Zionists and even anti-Zionists, the settlers themselves have contributed to the spread of that nihilistic post-Zionism now infecting Israeli society. The erosion of Zionist moral self-confidence on the part of large segments of the Israeli public begins with the misguided settlement project. The question is not whether the settlers are brave and idealistic but whether the settlement project contributes to or detracts from the values, goals, and aims of Zionism as it redefines itself in the 21st century.

The British Light Brigade was composed of men who were brave and idealistic beyond measure, but their famous charge was an example of colossal stupidity. General Lee's Confederate soldiers were brave and idealistic beyond measure, but that doesn't mean that Pickett's charge at Gettysburg was smart or that the cause they represented was sublime. One might wonder if Israel's settlement policy is not the political equivalent of the ill-fated British landing at Gallipoli in World War I, upon which the German Admiral De Robeck commented, "Gallant fellows, these soldiers; they always go for the thickest place in the fence." Israel's settlement policy compels Israeli diplomacy to always try to break through the thickest part of the diplomatic fence, the one and perhaps only place where Arab political superiority is manifest.

In political life, stupidity is the greatest sin, not immorality or illegality. Stupidity does greater harm to our fellow human beings than immorality. If we were to judge what is pro-Zionist and what is anti-Zionist according to their contribution to or their deleterious effect on Israel's economy, security, society, and overall morale and moral fortitude, we must conclude that the ideological settlements in the occupied territories constitute the most anti-Zionist activity conducted by any group of Jews since the advent of the Zionist project itself.

JEWISH PEASANTS AND WORKERS

Settlement policy was also connected to the social ideology of Labor Zionism which celebrated the Jewish return to agricultural activity and the creation of an industrial Jewish proletariat. This was called the "normalization" of the Jewish people and was perceived as having inherent ideological value. The political dominance of Labor Zionism from 1935 until 1977 and afterwards as sometimes ruling faction and sometimes major opposition inhibited a rational rethinking of settlement policy. It is certainly the case that agricultural settlements and basic labor-intensive industry (situated mainly in

Development Towns) served as the economic and social foundation for the establishment of the State. But in recent years labor intensive agricultural and industrial activities have had a mounting negative effect on Israel's economic, social, and environmental health.

Because agriculture has been celebrated as a primary value, and even as a metaphor for the return of the Jews to their ancient homeland, policy makers have been loath to take a hard and rational look at what agriculture really entails in 21st-century Israel. Israel has no water, and the Jews have no wish to work in a sector with such an abysmal pay scale. Today, water-poor Israel subsidizes the export of water (for that is what you are exporting when you export agricultural products) to water-rich Germany, France, and Scandinavia in order to create jobs for Thai guest workers – all in the name of Zionist values!

The justifications for labor-intensive industries are no less irrational and their consequences for Israel's economy and society no less detrimental. Ever since the Six-Day War, these industries have continued to survive only because of massive direct and indirect subsidies. Despite subsidies, pay scales in these labor-intensive industries have seldom exceeded minimum wage, even for people with years of seniority. These industries form the economic base of the Development Towns and thus have become major contributors to the deepening social/ethnic gap. One cannot have minimum wage industries and close the social gap. And one cannot close the social gap by simply raising the minimum wage by several hundred shekels. One can only close the social gap by raising the *median wage* and this cannot be done on the back of labor intensive industries. In a dynamic society such as Israel, the gap can only widen as long as such industries exist.

Labor-intensive industries require a large pool of low-income, low-skilled workers to compete in the global labor market. All the education budgets, welfare programs, and anti-poverty projects in the world cannot neutralize this basic negative economic and social dynamic. Mandating a slight increase in the minimum wage as a medicine for poverty is like peddling aspirin as a cure for chronic diseases. High-tech industries and sophisticated services, on the other hand, need a large pool of highly skilled and hence highly paid workers. This creates positive economic and social dynamics that can help close the social gap.

Even massive direct and indirect subsidies cannot keep Israel's labor-intensive industries alive. As with other developed countries, they are moving to third world countries. Israel has been experiencing desperate protests against closures by workers who have long been disgusted with their working conditions and wages. These workers want their factories to stay open because they have no other options, but would have preferred to work elsewhere. Consequently, Israel still has poverty, an even larger social gap, and an added "bonus" of chronic large-scale (up to 15%) unemployment in Development Towns.

The psychological and cultural consequences of this situation might be even more disturbing. A grinding frustration and bitterness and sense of wasting one's life hang like a terrible cloud over large numbers of Israel's population. People can sustain dreadful poverty when they feel they are engaged in a transcendent historical enterprise. The poverty and living conditions of the early *Halutzim* (pioneers) were immeasurably worse than the most impoverished segments of Israel's population today. But they were the vanguard of their people and of a great historical enterprise. Their poverty did not degrade them; indeed in some strange way it even uplifted them. They were at the pinnacle of Maslow's self-actualization and approaching Frankel's self-transcendence. Today's poverty, on the other hand is mind-deadening and soul-deadening. It is a poverty of hopelessness, while that of the *Halutzim* was a poverty of hopefulness.

In contrast to the unemployment figures in the Development Towns, the unemployment figures in the non-industrial, non-pioneering, non-proletariat Sharon area (Kfar Saba, Ra'anana, Herzlia), just north of Tel Aviv, are less than 3%. This area is a high-tech hotbed. Its sophisticated services and innovation contributes perhaps a billion dollars a year to Israel's export figures. Yet, according to classical Zionist conceptions, these towns have nowhere near the Zionist value that settlements or development towns or near bankrupt kibbutzim have.

The crisis of labor-intensive industries could have been avoided by applying the principles of *futurist thinking* and simple trend analysis. By the late 1970s, it was clear to anyone who cared to analyze the trends that labor-intensive industries had no future in the developed world. Intelligent policy makers in other developed countries began to get rid of their labor-intensive industries gradually, moving them to Hong Kong, South Korea, and Taiwan and later on to Thailand, Malaysia, and Indonesia, combining this economic policy with a major redirection of the educational system.

The gradual process of eliminating older workers, as they achieved retirement age, while not absorbing younger workers, led to drastically shrinking these work forces without social dislocation. Young people entering the work force were directed to other lines of work, or if already in the work force were retrained for other branches of the economy. Israeli policy makers, on the other hand, still infatuated with the ideological myth of the Jewish industrial worker and having no alternative answers for the Development Towns, failed to change course. The resultant social dislocation and trauma bear witness to the shortsighted foolishness of perpetuating this particular Zionist value long after its historical shelf life had expired.

Here the contradictions of the Zionist Left in particular are laid bare, the contradiction between a Zionist ideology that celebrates

Jews returning to physical labor and a socialist ideology of a decent living wage. These two ideologies have never been able to coexist.

THE DISENGAGEMENT

The Gaza disengagement is past us physically and practically. Yet it will persist in the Jewish world's political discourse. Let us attempt to clarify the reasons for this historic act in all its dimensions: the question of Jewish rights to the Land of Israel, the real alternatives facing any Israeli government vis-à-vis the occupied territories, the real cost of the settlements vis-à-vis the true tasks of Zionism, the complex security consequences of the decision and finally the question of whether it was democratic.

THE QUESTION OF HISTORICAL RIGHTS

David Ben Gurion once said that the Jewish people have an absolute moral and historical right to the entire Land of Israel but that we also have the right not to exercise this moral and historical right if it interferes with other more vital rights and needs of the Jewish people. This approach reflects the concept that the People of Israel is the hub of Zionism, not the Land of Israel; the people are the aim, the Land is the means. It implies that the Land only has moral value when it serves real Jewish persons and is devoid of moral value when it sacrifices the needs of Jewish persons.

Those that argue against any kind of territorial compromise often refer to past Talmudic prohibitions against this. They also refer to the sanctity inherent in the suffering of past generations. Our task in their minds is to use the future as a means to put into practice the principles of the past and not to use the past as an inspiration to create a different future. A rational, historically rooted but futurist oriented policy, however, would allow that the past has a voice but not a veto.

The Real Alternatives Facing Israel

1. Annex the territories and give all its inhabitants full rights as citizens. Consequence: the end of the Jewish State by democratic means.

2. Annex the territories and not give all its inhabitants full rights as citizens.
Consequence: Apartheid and the end of the Jewish State by international sanctions.

3. Annex the territories and "transfer" all of its inhabitants.
Consequence: Ethnic cleansing and the end of the Jewish State by international sanctions.

4. The disengagement

5. The status quo with all its deleterious implications (as noted above)

Security Consequences of the Disengagement

We must relate to the grand strategic, strategic, operational and tactical aspects of the disengagement:

Grand Strategy: the economic, political, military, social and moral resources of a people and how best to optimally mobilize them in order to minimize weaknesses and achieve *vital goals*. Grand strategy defines the criteria and priorities by which we determine policy goals; it is the filter through which we pass our policy goals to see if they are appropriate. In a sane and rational entity, grand strategy determines policy more than ideology. Ideology might strive for an ideal but in real life we must construct policies based upon reality. *The disengagement strengthened our grand strategic position immensely: politically, economically, morally and socially.*

Strategic threats: Strategic threats, as opposed to tactical threats, are those threats that endanger the very existence of the State. There are two fundamental existential threats to Israel as a Jewish State: Iran's nuclear weapons and Palestinian demographics. *The disengagement strengthened our strategic position by ridding us of one and half million Palestinians thus greatly lessening the demographic threat.*

Operational advantages: Operations has to do with the rational and most effective deployment of military assets in order to achieve a security aim. By removing the army from Gaza – and the requirement to defend 8,000 settlers in dozens of small communities – we have shortened our lines of defense and placed our armed forces along defensible borders. As I said above: diminishing concentrations of soldiers on longer lines of defense equals less security, while higher concentrations of soldiers on shorter lines of defense equals more security. *The disengagement strengthened our operational position by enabling a more rational deployment of military assets.*

Tactical: The Palestinians now have significantly greater freedom of movement and can bring their Kassam rockets closer to the border with Israel giving them a greater ability to fire on Israeli settlements within the green line. But Israel also has greater freedom of response to such attacks since we have withdrawn. *The disengagement may have weakened or strengthened our tactical position – we do not yet know. What we do know is that grand strategy, strategy and operations take precedence over tactics.*

THE QUESTION OF DEMOCRACY

Was the decision to disengage democratic and constitutional? Let us review the facts. A democratically elected government, exercising the State's sovereign right of *eminent domain*, decided to remove some of its citizens from a certain area and relocate them for the greater public good: that greater public good being the rationalizing of the lines of defense, weakening the demographic threat to Israel and improving our general standing in the world.

The government voted to endorse the plan and it was ratified by the Knesset. The decision was reviewed by the Supreme Court in regards to its legality and constitutionality. The Court overwhelmingly ruled in favor, with only one dissenting voice. The disengagement should be seen as the first minor step in an overall and comprehensive reevaluation of settlement policy. This would enable us to formulate more rational security, economic, social and political policies in the future.

| CHAPTER 6 |

THE FUTURE OF ARAB-JEWISH RELATIONS

A robust policy must have clearly defined first principles to sustain itself over time. The first principle pertaining to our relations with the Arabs should be what is good for the Jews. In its modern context, this means what is good for Zionism. I have already defined Zionism as the collective option for individual Jews in Israel or in the Diaspora to integrate into modern life without sacrificing their Jewish identity. I do not define Zionism as the attempt to recreate the Kingdom of David, reconstruct the Temple, with attendant animal sacrifice, or construct a settlement everywhere the patriarch Abraham once rested his head.

We should want peace because it is good for the Jews, not because self-appointed humanitarians will love us or because it will relieve accumulated Arab stress at being consistently defeated by the lowly Jew. I identify myself with the first generation of Jews without inherent guilt; I do not open my eyes in the morning and say, "We are guilty," and then ask what we are guilty of.

I want peace because Jews will no longer be killed, Israel's economy will prosper, tourism will rejuvenate, unemployment will decrease, our democracy will grow stronger, and the standards of our civil service will approach European levels. I do not want peace in order to win the Nobel Prize or to go to heaven. I do not consider peace the most important thing in human affairs. Survival is more important, security is more important, liberty is more important, justice is more important, freedom is more important, dignity and honor are more important, and constitutional democracy is more important. I am not willing to sacrifice any of the above in order to achieve peace.

I am for a peace that increases Israel's security, its international political status, and its economic strength, thus enabling Israel to close the social ethnic gap. I believe in taking calculated *tactical* risks in order to achieve the above. I do not believe in taking *strategic* risks, calculated or otherwise. Any call for Jews to sacrifice or even risk sacrificing their vital interests in the name of peace should be rejected (self-sacrifice being the most grotesque form of human sacrifice).

I know that to achieve peace we must take into consideration the Palestinian concern for security, national liberty, justice, dignity, and honor. I know that we have not always paid proper respect to Palestinian concerns about these issues and that many Jews in Israel and the Diaspora have nothing but contempt for the aspirations of Palestinians. I distance myself from these people, not to gain international praise but because to achieve peace we must recognize and accommodate, to the best of our ability, *legitimate* Palestinian aspirations.

THE PEACE PROCESS AND SETTLEMENTS

These views explain why, despite the second *Intifada*, I affirm the Madrid/Oslo process as being the crucial Zionist achievement of the 1990s.

The Madrid/Oslo process raised Israel's international political standing and helped contribute to the robust economic growth of Israel throughout the 1990s. Israel's economy is export driven and during the 1990s 60% of Israel's export growth was to countries and markets we had not traded with prior to the Madrid/Oslo process. This economic growth was a major reason for the relatively successful absorption of close to one million immigrants from the former Soviet Union. These immigrants supplied close to 50% of Israel's technical manpower needs during the 1990s. Their availability was a major cause for increased foreign investment in Israel's technology sectors which, despite its inherent volatility, is the basis for future economic growth.

Another positive consequence of the Madrid/Oslo process was the breakdown of the Arab boycott, which had for some time been losing its effectiveness as Israel's relative economic power grew and the relative economic influence of Arab oil power waned. The weakening of the boycott removed the final psychological barrier to international investment in Israel which grew substantially in the 1990s.

The Madrid/Oslo process was, therefore, a major contributor to Israel's economy growing by 40% and its Jewish population growing by 25% during the 1990s. Madrid/Oslo has been good for the Jews, notwithstanding the failure to achieve a final peace or the subsequent outbreak of violence. We had seven years of violence before Oslo, several years of violence during Oslo, and there is no reason to assume that the second *Intifada* could have been avoided if we had not concluded Oslo. Oslo provided Israel with an opportunity to realize strategic Zionist aims even while opening Israel up to severe tactical challenges that, while murderous and intolerable, do not present any real strategic dangers to Israel's existence. On balance, Oslo has been a Zionist achievement.

The existence of the ideological settlements forecloses options for interim (unilateral) separation from or a final settlement with the Palestinians. Either option would be beneficial to Israel and the Jewish people. These settlements constitute a Gordian knot that we are constantly trying to untie, with endless bypass roads and tunnels and overpasses as well as costly security arrangements that divert Israel's military assets away from areas of better use. The operational and logistic shortcomings of the second Lebanese War can be attributed, in large measure, to this misdirection of military assets.

A perverse logic is at work here. Many Israelis and Diaspora Jews assume that because the settlements are so obnoxious to the Arabs they must be good for the Jews. We have not considered that the settlements might be both obnoxious to the Arabs and dysfunctional to Jewish interests. Anything so harmful to Zionism, to our relationship with Arab countries and the world should be vigorously combated on purely Zionist grounds. A first step must be the unilateral removal of mini-settlements (unauthorized *and* authorized) located in a sea of hostile Arabs. Such a step would create maneuvering room for Israel, enabling it to take unilateral steps if future negotiations with the Palestinians do not bear fruit. Ironically, these settlements serve the Palestinian political cause because they limit Israel's freedom of action, making it dependent on Palestinian agreement. That is why sophisticated Palestinian militants opposed the disengagement. The removal of the settlements does not necessarily mean removing the army or ending the occupation. Until there is a final peace arrangement I would oppose this. What it does is to allow a more efficient use of military assets – instead of guarding settlements the army would be able to concentrate on rooting out and intercepting terrorists, and destroying the terror infrastructure.

FUTURE RELATIONS WITH THE ARAB WORLD

Jewish relations with the Arabs must be fair but firm, with an unconditional demand for reciprocity. What we should demand from ourselves regarding the Arabs we must demand from the Arabs regarding ourselves. Without fairness, we will not achieve peace.

Without firmness, we will not prevail. Radical hawks and radical doves are equally mistaken.

Firmness refers not only to military firmness, but to a reciprocal moral standard. The attitudes of the Israeli Left in particular have often been too forgiving. Because peace means so much to them, they have often overlooked corruption, incompetence, and racism in Arab countries as well as in many self-governing bodies of Israel's own Arab citizens. This misplaced tolerance must cease. We must adopt a policy of zero tolerance for Arab corruption and racism as well as their dismissive contempt for legitimate Jewish rights. A great moral failure of the Israeli Left has been its ultra-sensitivity and criticism of Jewish contempt for legitimate Arab rights and concerns, while overlooking the much greater Arab contempt for Jewish rights and concerns – indeed, contempt for the Jews per se.

Toward the Arab and Moslem world in general, we must become proactive, unapologetic lobbyists to end direct and indirect international funding to countries, projects, and educational systems that dissemimate anti-Semitic propaganda and that implement racist policies. We must become proactive in publicizing attitudes toward women in these countries. We must demand of the world and of ourselves a single standard. We may not succeed, but at least we will expose these activities and norms. This will help neutralize the posture of moral superiority of anti-Israeli propagandists, which puts so many Israeli and Jewish spokespeople on the defensive. We must force the Arabs to explain their behavior and actions and change the present state of affairs wherein we Jews are constantly forced to explain ours.

CAN ISRAEL BE A JEWISH AND DEMOCRATIC STATE?

Israel is a Jewish *and* a democratic state. Democracy for Israel is not just some abstract ideal – it is an absolute necessity. Israel would not earn the support of the United States and of American and European Jewry if we were like other Middle Eastern countries. We must reject the claim of Jewish extremists that either we are a Jewish state or a democratic state and that as long as we are at war we cannot afford the luxury of democracy. It is precisely because we are at war and require powerful democratic allies, that we must remain democratic.

We must also reject the attempts of Arab intellectuals as well as post-Zionist Jewish intellectuals to de-Zionize and de-Judaize the state by changing the national anthem, *Hatikvah*, and removing symbols such as the Star of David and the menorah. We must emphatically and unapologetically reject the demand that Israel become a state of all its citizens *instead* of a Jewish state. Israel can and must be both. Israel *can* and *must* be both a Jewish and a democratic state. If either of these components is removed from the equation, neither Israel nor the Jewish people will have a meaningful future.

THE IMPORTANCE OF SYMBOLS

The demand of Arab nationalists and Jewish post-Zionists to remove the Star of David from the Israeli flag as well as to replace the menorah as the national emblem and *HaTikvah* as the national anthem must be rejected. This demand does not reflect superior moral and democratic values. It reflects the residual historical contempt of Christianity and Islam for any Jewish pretension at political equality as well as the habitual obsequiousness of a certain breed of Jewish intellectual.

England, Norway, Finland, Denmark, Sweden, Greece, Iceland, and Switzerland are all democratic countries, and all have Christian crosses in their national flags. Most have an official state religion. England and Denmark are structural theocracies: the Queen is head of the Anglican Church in England, and the Parliament has ultimate control of the Lutheran Church in Denmark. These countries' national mythologies, coats of arms, and holidays are not ethnically neutral; they reflect the dominant ethnic group, even while conferring freedom and equality to all their citizens, whatever their ethnicity. In this sense, Denmark is the country of the Lutheran Danes and of all its citizens, and no Jew or Moslem residing in Denmark or deracinated Danish intellectual would dare demand the removal of the cross from the flag.

India is the largest democracy in the world. Its flag has an ancient Hindu symbol, the *dharma chakra*, at its center, just as the Star of David is at the center of Israel's flag. The state emblem of India is a representation of the top of a pillar built by *Asoka*, a Hindu who converted to Buddhism, just as the state emblem of Israel is a menorah. Some 20% of India's population is non-Hindu and non-Buddhist, with more than 150 million Moslems and close to 20 million Christians whose rights as citizens are also constitutionally guaranteed. Could one imagine these non-Hindus attempting to carry on a public campaign to change the symbols of India?

India's non-Hindus justifiably fight to translate their *formal* constitutional rights into equal treatment in *practice*. Israel's Arabs should also fight to translate their formal constitutional rights into equal treatment in practice and not constantly accuse the Jews of racism because we desire one geographically insignificant state on the face of the planet whose national symbols are Jewish. By so doing Israeli Arabs would earn the support of many Jews; but it is psychologically difficult to fight for the equal *civil* rights of people who deny you equal *national* rights.

Israel's democratic model is Denmark, not the United States. Denmark should be a *light unto the Jews*, and we should strive to equal Denmark in its treatment of its non-Lutheran non-Danish population. We certainly do not want our models to be Pakistan, Algeria, Libya, Mauritania, or Tunisia, all of which contain the Islamic crescent in their flags, a fact that for some reason does not excite the indignation of European, Moslem, or deracinated Jewish intellectuals as being racist.

THE LAW OF RETURN

And what of the Law of Return? How can a country that pretends to be democratic have a basic immigration law that favors one ethnic group over all others? Is this not a racist law by definition? In an imaginary world of absolutes, it might be so. In the real world of imperfect, empirical, historical context, it is the opposite of racism. In this real world, the Law of Return is a humanistic response to racism.

In its original formulation, the Law of Return guaranteed a safe haven for anyone who would have been exterminated as a Jew by Hitler. This included numerous individuals who had no self-definition or even self-knowledge that they had Jewish antecedents and were by definition not even Jews according to Jewish tradition. This makes it a real stretch of the imagination to call this a racist law – especially since it came in response to the "civilized" world's failure to offer safe haven during the Nazi period. The countries of the West closed their borders, sentencing hundreds of thousands if not millions of Jews and others to death. For so-called intellectuals and humanists to attack as racist this most human and humane response to the moral failure of their own societies is an example of moral and intellectual dishonesty of immense proportions. For Jewish intellectuals to do so is an example of politically correct toadying reflecting a complete lack of self-respect.

But the Law of Return also has moral and historical justification independent of the Holocaust. It is an example of political affirmative action, which should not in itself offend politically correct postmodernists. The Jews suffered for 2,000 years because they had no safe geographical/political haven in which they had demographic, political, cultural, and economic hegemony. Zionism was born well before the Holocaust and is not dependent on the Holocaust for its justification. Zionism is dedicated to correcting the condition of Jewish disenfranchisement by creating and sustaining a Jewish state in which the Jewish people are able to guarantee their demographic, political, cultural, and economic hegemony. The Law of Return is an integral and necessary part of this guarantee, and its basic moral assumptions are similar to various affirmative action laws and programs in the West. When a minority is discriminated against over a long historical period in a vital area of human activities, they must be allowed to claim certain privileges to repair the damage. The Law of Return fits this definition and is, therefore, morally justified and by definition not racist. It is rather a mechanism to correct the racist inheritance of thousands of years of anti-Semitism.

It is interesting to note how many other countries in the world have similar laws and ponder why these do not arouse the indignation of international moralists. The following is a *partial* list:

1. Armenia: the *Declaration* on *Independence of Armenia* declares that "Armenians living abroad are entitled to the citizenship of the Republic of Armenia".

2. China: Chinese immigration law gives priority to returning ethnic Chinese. The term Overseas Chinese may be defined narrowly to

refer only to people of Han ethnicity.

3. Finland: The *Finnish Aliens Act* provides for persons who are of Finnish origin to receive permanent residence.

4. Germany: German law allows persons of German descent living in Eastern Europe to return to Germany and acquire German citizenship.

5. India: (citizenship) is available to persons of Indian origin anywhere in the world as long as they have never been citizens of Pakistan or of Bangladesh.

6. Ireland: *Irish Nationality Law* provides for Irish citizenship to be acquired on the basis of at least one Irish grandparent. If a person outside of Ireland who is entitled to claim Irish citizenship elects not to, that person may nonetheless pass that right on to her or his own children, even if the basis for the entitlement passed on is a single Irish grandparent.

7. Lithuania: the *Constitution of Lithuania* states: "Every Lithuanian person may settle in Lithuania."

8. Poland: the *Constitution of Poland*, states: "Anyone whose Polish origin has been confirmed in accordance with statute may settle permanently in Poland."

9. Spain: Sephardi Jews, from wherever in the world, can claim Spanish citizenship. (Interesting that Spain can have a Law of Return for Jews but Israel cannot.)

10. Taiwan: Taiwan's immigration law gives priority to ethnic Chinese and encourages their return.

Other countries have similar laws. They all reflect a desire by various governments to guarantee a safe haven to Diaspora populations, particularly those assumed to be living under precarious conditions. Why are they any different from the Israeli Law of Return?

JEWISH ATTITUDES TOWARD ISRAELI ARABS

In regards to Israeli Arabs, we must adopt a creative policy based upon justice and equality before the law, nondiscrimination in the job market, and equal access to public budgets. But what should be our response to Israeli Arab leaders and intellectuals who call for the de-Judaizing of Israel? In my view we must say that Israel's democracy permits any Israeli citizen to call for the destruction of the Jewish State by way of erasing all of its Jewish symbols. But this same democracy also enables us Jews to refrain from cooperating with those who deny the Jewish national right to a state founded on Jewish symbols and Jewish culture.

Israeli Arabs should always have equal rights and privileges under Israel's democratic form of government and should not be discriminated against in Israeli courts or in regards to public budgets. Those Israeli Arabs or leaders who support the notion that Israel should cease to be a Jewish state, however, should not expect active civil or political cooperation from self-respecting Jews. For self-respecting democratic Jews, Israel's Arab citizens have four options:

1. To fight for equal implementation of laws and budgets within the framework of the Jewish State. If this is the chosen option, many democratic Jews will be their active partners.
2. To continue to call for the destruction of the Jewish State, in which case respect for Arab rights will be completely passive and formal and Israeli Arabs will forego active cooperation from Jewish civil

or political society. The status of Israeli Arabs who embrace such a position will be much the same as Louis Farrakhan's Nation of Islam or the Aryan Brotherhood in the United States: freedom of speech and assembly, yes, acceptance and cooperation, no.

3. Voluntary emigration from Israel if its particular Jewish character is so odious to them. This is an acceptable option: many English speakers have moved from francophone Quebec, not because their constitutional rights have been endangered but because they felt uncomfortable and not completely at home in French culture and society. Others have remained, adapted, and compromised. This same democratic option holds for those of Israel's Arab citizens who cannot stomach the thought of living in a Jewish state. This option is in no way comparable to the controversial *transfer* policy advocated by certain segments of Israel's radical right wing. No Israeli Arab would be "encouraged" to leave the country. Voluntary emigration, on the other hand, is an option for every citizen, Jewish or Arab. Indeed about a half million Jewish citizens have emigrated because various aspects of Israeli society did not suit them. This same option is open to Israel's Arab citizens.

4. To receive *complete* (not cultural) autonomy in areas presently under the jurisdiction of local Arab Councils. Those Israeli Arabs who opt for autonomy will cease to be Israeli citizens and will lose the right to vote for Israel's Knesset. They will vote for their own Arab Agency (analogous to the Jewish Agency), with its own flag, symbols, and hymn, which will generate its own educational and development budgets and coordinate with the Jewish State by way of a common development authority which will deal with issues such as access to Israel's highway, water, electrical, and sewage systems and the fees the Arab Agency will pay to the state for its share in their use. The Knesset, as the sovereign legislative body of the state, has the authority to pass laws rescinding Israeli

sovereignty over areas with a substantial Arab or Jewish population. I mention Jewish because it is clear to many Israelis that in the near future, whether through peace or unilateral withdrawal, the Knesset will be forced to rescind sovereignty over most of East Jerusalem and the Golan Heights. The West Bank never having been annexed will not require a similar legal procedure.

5. Another alternative open to Israeli Arabs, as communities or as individuals, would be annexation to the Palestinian state, even in areas noncontiguous to the Palestinian state, thus becoming Palestinian citizens. If groups or individuals of Israeli Arabs opt for either one of these two options, the Jews will respect their choice – just as Slovakia's decision to separate from the Czechs was respected. None of this will prejudice the constitutional rights of those Arabs who choose to remain citizens of the Jewish State.

Arab Corruption, Sexism and Racism

Whenever the call for equality of budgets for Arabs is raised in Israel, we typically see a wave of Jewish authored articles describing in detail the astounding corruption and administrative incompetence of Israeli Arab municipalities. The point of these articles is that before more money is funneled into the Arab sector we should guarantee higher standards of public behavior and transparency vis-à-vis public budgets dedicated to that sector.

Zero tolerance for these phenomena, as well as for the status of women in the Arab sector, are indeed moral imperatives. Excusing or overlooking these negative phenomena in the name of brotherhood and tolerance is politically correct multiculturalism gone wild. But we Jews should not hasten to adopt a stance of moral superiority. We encouraged and nurtured the traditional corruption of the Arab sector. Let us name it *mukhtarism*, after the traditional name for local Arab leadership, the *mukhtar*. We made the traditional corrupt leadership of the Arab communities our conduit to our Arab citizens rather than encouraging the development of modern concepts of citizenship, civic behavior and the status of Arab women.

This has led to a situation contrary to the interests of the Zionist project. The inferior status of Arab women has produced a serious demographic challenge to Jews in Israel. The inferior level of Arab public administration and services has resulted in bitterness, which has indirectly contributed to radical tendencies in Israel's Arab citizens.

The irony is that, despite our best efforts to prevent it, a new militant Israeli Arab parliamentary leadership has arisen. Their attitudes are semi-modern but cynical and bitter, with no great desire to encourage higher standards of citizenship in the Arab sector. Rather than engage in critical analyses of the effects of *mukhtarism* on Israeli Arab society, which might reflect a genuine concern for Israeli Arab welfare, they cynically exploit its consequences for their own political agenda in order to build their own political power. The Israeli Arab parliamentary lobby, rather than alleviating Israeli Arab distress through a combination of internal reform and external lobbying, has an interest in exacerbating this distress to generate the extremism necessary for their real agenda: support for the still vigorous dream of a Greater Palestine.

THE FUTURE

Future policy should incorporate the following:

1. Affirmative action programs for Israeli Arab women in every area of Israeli life: education, advancement in public positions, hostels for battered Israeli Arab women, boarding schools for Arab girls being "socially abused" by their fathers by being kept out of school, etc.

2. Recognition of a Palestinian state and a rejection of the *current* interpretation of United Nations Resolution 194 calling for the repatriation of Palestinian refugees to their original homes. Accepting this interpretation would be tantamount to the suicide of the Jewish State.

3. Total rejection of double standards in regards to the norms of governance in the Israeli Arab sector as well as in Arab countries.

4. Reevaluation of the Israeli Arab job market. This means the active enlistment of skilled Israeli Arabs in public sector positions.

Such a policy would combine Jewish self-esteem with social justice for the Arab population and would reflect the fact that Israel is not only a Jewish state but also a democratic state with concern for all its citizens.

CHAPTER 7

LIVING WITH THE CHRISTIANS

The Jewish Diaspora resides in Christian and post-Christian countries. Israel's two most important relationships are with the United States and the European Union. Consequently the near future of the Jewish people is tied to Christian and post-Christian societies. So even though Israel strives to integrate into the Moslem Middle East and to develop close connections with India, China and Japan, Jewry's relationship with "Christendom" should be a primary concern.

Today it is the seductive power of *uncritical* ecumenism and the glib cliché of "all 'religions' are really the same" that challenge the Jewish future, not inquisitions, pogroms, and holocausts. 'Religion' is in quotation marks because Judaism, like Confucianism, is as much a life system as it is a religion in the Christian sense. I believe the terms Jewish tradition, Jewish worldview, or Jewish ideology convey a truer sense of Jewishness than the term Jewish 'religion'.

This is not just an exercise in semantics. The future of Jewish-Christian relations must be based upon a reaffirmation of Jewish cultural particularity and the end of Jewish apologetics. We Jews are the minority and are obliged to be unambiguous regarding our differences with Christianity. Ecumenism does not mean the blurring of differences for fear of offending those with a different view of life, or shading our view of the world in order to be socially acceptable and immune to physical and political intimidation.

This requires a 21st century reaffirmation of the Enlightenment principle of separation between church and state. Enlightenment principles are not the enemy of modern Jewish identity and survival, as some neo-Orthodox thinkers now claim; they are a prerequisite for continued Jewish identity and survival.

Ecumenism should simply mean good planetary citizenship based on the same principles as the American republic: freedom of inquiry and freedom of conscience. These principles require us not to murder one another or harm one another because we have different views of the world. We can and should cooperate with Christians and adherents of other faiths and philosophical outlooks as responsible citizens of our respective countries and of the planet. But the "ecumenical" blurring of differences is creating Jewish indifference to the Jewish tradition.

We should be mindful, however, that today most Christians of whatever denomination are indifferent to doctrinal issues and are content to conduct respectful relationships with Jews (and one another) outside a theological frame of reference. I hope, therefore, that what follows does not in anyway inhibit or damage the fruitful Christian-Jewish cooperation of the past 50 years.

JUDEO-CHRISTIAN ETHIC: MYTH AND REALITY

What is similar and what is different between the Jewish worldview and the Christian worldview? With clarity comes understanding, and with understanding comes mutual respect. Judaism and Christianity are in general agreement about many moral principles regarding human life. It is in the moral living of life on a daily basis that we discover significant differences.

Jews and Christians accept the Ten Commandments as the foundation of morality. So do the Moslems. Buddhists, Confucians,

Shintoists, and animistic religions also have similar moral principles. This is a practical requirement of civilization. Human beings must live in society to survive. To do so, they must not murder one another nor steal from one another etc. For this practical reason, all great religions and philosophical systems have similar moral principles.

Christians and Moslems accept the Jewish maxim that human beings are created in the image of God, are equal in "his" eyes, and inherently valuable as individuals. This belief is particular to monotheistic religions. This would be a Judeo-Christian-Islamic ethic.

If human beings are valuable in themselves, their lives are valuable and have meaning. If they are created in the image of God, they have natural rights that no earthly power can take away. These are called *inalienable rights*. Individuals are sanctified for having been made in the image of God. In its secularized form, the concept of individual sanctity has served as the basis for resistance to tyranny as well as for constitutional protections of individual rights.

SOME DIFFERENCES BETWEEN JUDAISM AND CHRISTIANITY

At the every day level of moral decision making the "Judeo-Christian ethic" is frequently a phrase without genuine meaning. Comparative perspectives on abortion and altruism versus egoism highlight this.

Jews justify abortion when the fetus threatens the life of the mother on the grounds of self-defense. This is in accord with the Talmudic dictum, "He who comes to kill you, arise and kill him first." In the Jewish tradition, self-defense is a moral *obligation*, not a moral right, even regarding an unborn fetus. Such argumentation is alien to Christianity, but it is a concrete expression of a first principle of Judaism: the unconditional right to our own lives.

On the other hand, the Christian ideal is to be Christ-like, to constantly ask what Jesus would have done. What Jesus did was to sacrifice himself so that humanity could be purified of sin and be saved.

The Christian ethical structure is based upon the most famous case of altruism in human history, someone unconditionally giving up his life for others. I would not presume to challenge the spiritual or therapeutic power of the crucifixion story for believing Christians or the positive role it played in civilizing barbarian Europe. I would only say that it cannot be accommodated into a Jewish belief system. A Jew cannot be a Jew and be for the Jesus of the crucifixion story. Jews would view *unconditional* self-sacrifice as an incongruous form of human sacrifice. Judaism forbids one to engage in reckless altruism that threatens one's life.

This Jewish ideal is demonstrated by a famous Talmudic case: *Mayim Le Shtaim* (water for two). A modern version of this story would go like this:

Two individuals have to cross a dry desert. Their survival depends on each of them taking two full canteens of water, the minimum needed to survive the crossing; anything less than two full canteens means certain death. At the point of no return and after they have each consumed one canteen, one of them discovers that he forgot to fill his second canteen. What is the moral obligation of the individual who remembered to fill both canteens? Remember, if he shares his remaining canteen with his forgetful friend he too will surely die.

A believing Christian, whose personal ideal is to be Christ-like, will almost certainly share his remaining water and pray to God that they will both be spared. He will risk sacrificing himself in order to be like Christ, placing his life in the hands of fate and faith. The rabbis who discussed this case, however, concluded that not only was the responsible person not morally obligated to share his water with the irresponsible person; it would be a moral transgression if he did so.

In the Jewish tradition, a responsible person has no moral obligation to risk sacrificing his life because an irresponsible person has placed himself in danger. Judaism celebrates the heroism of the soldier sacrificing himself for his comrades or the parent for the child but does not obligate us to sacrifice our lives as a *condition* for justifying our lives. If our very existence causes suffering to other beings, we have the moral obligation to try to ameliorate that suffering, but we have no obligation or moral right to sacrifice ourselves in order to relieve that suffering.

SUPERFICIAL ECUMENISM

The Judeo-Christian ethic has become a fashionable phrase in recent years because of a shallow ecumenism which hides underlying considerations. I believe Christians use this phrase for positive and negative reasons.

Positive: Since the Holocaust, Christians have recognized how Christian anti-Semitism contributed to the greatest crime in human annals. This realization horrified them as human beings and as Christians because it endangered the foundational bedrock of Christianity as a religion of love. By stressing the common ethical bond, they wanted to demonstrate the similarities of the two religions thereby heading off manifestations of anti-Semitism amongst their own future co-religionists. It was a sincere attempt after the fact to make amends.

Negative: The *Jews for Jesus* and *Messianic Jews* use this phrase as a strategy for breaking down Jewish resistance to their proselytizing efforts by way of Jewish symbols. They argue their case in the following way: "our ethical view of the world is the same, we are not asking you to give up your Jewish culture, all we are doing is adding on

Jesus who himself was a practicing Jew. You are not losing anything, or changing anything, you are only gaining spiritual added value."

Belief in Jesus as personal savior and the feeling of being born again and liberated from past sins has tremendous psychological appeal and therapeutic value for those who have led a life of troubles or anti-social and self-destructive behavior. Therefore, this method of argument and proselytizing strategy has had some success in the Jewish community.

The Jews, on the other hand, use the term Judeo-Christian ethic because it can be used to defuse potential anti-Semitism. It not only provides an ideological shield against future hostility it signifies acceptance into Christian society.

SOME PRIMARY JEWISH PRINCIPLES

Judaism is characterized by several principles that clarify some differences with Christianity.

THE WAR AGAINST IDOLATRY

The worship of anything that can be conceived of in a material or bodily sense would be considered idolatry for Jews. The very attempt to define or materialize or personalize God is idolatrous for the Jew.

THE INHERENT INABILITY TO POSITIVELY DEFINE THE CONCEPT OF "GOD"

The expression "I believe in God' is problematic for Jews who understand the essence of Judaism, even though belief in the existence of God is the first of the 613 commandments. To utter that sentence, They would first require a clear, objective definition of what God is and then clarify what they mean by belief. Here we must refer back to Maimonides' *negative theology* – that is, what we cannot say about God – as an alternative to Christian *positive theology*, the attempt to describe the nature of God.

Moses says to the "voice" emanating from the burning bush: "They (the People of Israel) will say unto me: what is his name? What shall I say unto them?" The common translation of God's reply is "I am who I am" or "I am that I am". A more precise translation would be "I will be what I will be" [an indefinite formulation, implying incompleteness: in biblical Hebrew it is the *imperfect* tense and in Modern Hebrew the *future* tense] ... say unto the children of Israel: 'I will be' hath sent me unto you ... this is my name forever ... my memorial unto all generations".

THE UNMEDIATED INDIVIDUAL CONNECTION WITH GOD

This is not a *personal* relationship with God. One cannot have a personal relationship with something that is not a person and that is beyond definition. What cannot be defined cannot be mediated, neither by a rabbi nor a priest nor Jesus. A Jew might have an intimate "relationship" with his own idea or sense of what God might be. He might even "appeal to him,", "praise him," "talk to him," "argue with him," or even "reprimand him," but a Jew cannot have a *personal* relationship with God.

A STRESS ON RIGHT ACTION RATHER THAN RIGHT BELIEF

Jews most often ask "do you keep the commandments?" and only rarely "do you believe in God?" The defining characteristic of the Jew is proper behavior not proper belief. No matter what the differences between the various trends of Judaism, all would agree that Judaism is behavior centered. Jews dispute about what acts and which commandments – not about which beliefs.

A classic Jewish story exemplifies this tradition. A yeshiva student approaches the head of the yeshiva in an attitude of trepidation and distress. "Rabbi I have a terrible problem." "What is your problem, my son?" "I no longer am able to believe in God." The rabbi ponders this astounding news and responds: "All right, but what has that to do with *yiddishkeit*?" In other words, what has that to do with being a good Jew? Would such an answer be possible for a believing Christian?

THE MORAL SOVEREIGNTY AND AUTONOMY OF THE INDIVIDUAL

The essence of Judaism is that people have absolute responsibility over their own lives. Jews cannot blame an outside force (the Devil) for bad behavior or look to an outside force (Jesus) to sanction or forgive behavior. "Bar Mitzvah" is the Jewish coming of age as an adult responsible for his or her behavior. To be adult means to exercise autonomous reason and to take responsibility for the rest of your life.

Catholics are forgiven their sins (against God and against man) in confession; Protestants are forgiven or cleansed of their sins (against God and against man), literally, born again, when they are saved. On Yom Kippur, Jews are forgiven *only* for their transgressions against God. They cannot be forgiven by God for sins against other people but only by those people themselves.

The Jewish God could be an absolute monarch, but has become a constitutional monarch ruling over autonomous individuals with certain inalienable rights – even vis-à-vis God. This is exemplified by the remarkable Talmudic story of Rabbi Eliezer trying to convince his colleagues of the justice of his position by calling on God. When a heavenly voice declared that Eliezer was right, Rabbi Jeremiah, representing the opposition majority opinion, responded that "*Torah was given to us on Sinai, and hence we have no need to pay heed to a heavenly voice.*" In other words, when autonomous human beings are discussing the rights and wrongs of an issue God has no place in the discussion. God seems to have agreed with this because according to the rest of the story: "He laughed [with joy], he replied, saying, 'My sons have defeated Me, My sons have defeated Me.'" What in the fundamental Christian worldview could accommodate the ethos that underlies this story? Does this story reflect a Judeo-Christian ethic?

PERSONAL ETHICS VERSUS GRACE

The concept that another has died for us and cleansed us of our sins; that we are now "saved" (forgiven) by an act of grace unrelated to personal behavior, is foreign to the entire Jewish worldview. One cannot be a Jew and believe in Jesus as one's personal savior. Such a belief is contrary to everything the Jewish tradition represents. Salvation for the Jew is not a gift of God; it is a reward that is earned. This renders "Jews for Jesus" a philosophical contradiction in terms.

SUBLIMINAL AND SUBVERSIVE ATTACKS ON JEWISH IDENTITY

Western society has inherited from its Christian roots a subliminal background music that implies the primitiveness of Judaism and remains essentially anti-Jewish. Innumerable negative images of Judaism that endanger Jewish identity have insinuated themselves into modern secular civilization. Examples of these are:

1. "Talmudic thinking" as derogatory
2. Jesus driving out the moneychangers as a legitimate purifying act in defiance of a degenerate and corrupt religious establishment
3. Tribal Judaism versus catholic (universal) Christianity
4. Legalistic Judaism versus Christian love

The inertia of these Christian views of Judaism continues in secular academic scholarship. Modern secular literature, history, and philosophy texts abound with such subtle pejoratives. They constitute cultural and psychological guerilla warfare against the poorly schooled modern Jew. They predispose him against his roots and a reuniting with these roots.

The famous historian Arnold Toynbee, relying on grotesque misrepresentations of Judaism inherited from Christianity, called the Jews a "fossil" whose historical relevance had ended with the appearance of Jesus and Christianity. This was presented as an objective historical analysis but was really a secular version of the Christian belief that with the advent of Christianity, Judaism ceased being a vigorous self-sufficient culture. Such intellectual fare has been fed to several generations of university trained Jews, alienating them from Jewish identity.

We Jews have been remiss in developing ways to combat these attacks on Jewish consciousness, partly because combating them is like combating a false rumor. How do we assert our cultural integrity in repelling the missionary assault of some Christians without offending our Christian and post-Christian allies and weakening our political position? Israel's biggest supporters in American civil society are the 70 million-strong Evangelical communities, the same communities that fund the various manifestations of the *Jews for Jesus* or *Messianic Jews*. This is a difficult strategic dilemma, but difficulty does not free us from our moral obligation to deal with it.

TALMUDIC THINKING VERSUS NEW TESTAMENT THINKING

Talmudic hairsplitting is a recognized pejorative even in secular debate; signifying a tortured, artificial style of argumentation. The Jews call this process *pilpul*, from the Hebrew word for pepper, because it sharpens the mind. Yet, if we were to critically examine Christian teaching, we might conclude that New Testament thinking could replace Talmudic thinking to indicate tortured, twisted, artificial logic. As shown below, scores of *Christian* intellectuals and scholars have been documenting this for years. A future Jewish educational project might be to prepare popular handbooks showing how Christian scholarship has often misinterpreted the Old Testament.

This would obligate us to reevaluate our own attitudes toward concepts like *pilpul*, which is often used as a pejorative even in Jewish circles. *Pilpul* is designed to train the minds of practitioners never to accept face value and always to seek new ways of thinking. Its misuse by ignorant rabbis to confuse and control the unschooled has given it a bad name. In point of fact, *pilpul* anticipated today's creative-thinking workshops, which train people to develop their lateral (associative) thinking by connecting and integrating concepts that appear unrelated. While *pilpul's* intent is to sharpen the mind, New Testament argumentation intends to prove the truth of Christianity and its claim to cosmic exclusivity. It is not an exercise – it is a foundation stone.

Over the past 100 years of critical Christian scholarship, many Catholic and Protestant scholars have questioned the veracity and factualness of much New Testament argumentation. For a remarkable description of this phenomenon, read *Jesus Son of Man* (Urizon Books, 1977) by Rudolf Augstein, founder and publisher of the German magazine *Der Spiegel*. Mr. Augstein, a non-Jew, has conducted secondary research into the writings of Catholic and Protestant scholars regarding the veracity of traditional Christian dogma. He documents their discoveries, highlights their reticence to bring these discoveries to light and severely criticizes what he construes to be intellectual dishonesty. His work has great relevance for Jews who want to reevaluate their tradition as it has been filtered through Christian eyes.

JESUS AND THE MONEY CHANGERS

In his first inaugural address, Franklin Delano Roosevelt referred to driving the moneychangers from the Temple. He was using this phrase as a metaphor for the control that American business tycoons had over the temple of American democracy. The image was immediately accessible to all Americans who even had a passing acquaintance with the New Testament. It is one of the most striking images of the entire Christ story and is universally recognized as a purifying and revolutionary act.

It is also a story that reinforces images of the Jew as a moneygrubber willing to pollute his own holiest of holies for profit. The entire Jesus/moneychanger story is seen through the retroactive filter of a medieval Christian view of the Jews. Jews have trouble dealing with this story because, at first glance, it seems like a just and noble revolutionary act, and many Jews feel shame that this was part of Temple activity. This comes from seeing the story through Christian eyes. Seeing the story from both a Jewish and modern point of view might change one's perspective.

First, we must relate to the Christian concept of the Temple as a quiet, dignified place of prayer and meditation being polluted by filthy commerce; a kind of cathedral, which people enter in quiet awe. In fact, the Temple was oriental. Whoever has visited the Far East or seen documentaries will recognize the noise, tumult, crowds, people hawking religious artifacts, animals walking around, women nursing, and perhaps even people willing to change money. A similar atmosphere was to be found in medieval European cathedrals.

Jews made pilgrimage to the Temple three times a year. These pilgrimages provided much of the income of Jerusalem residents. Jews came from long distances, often with their families. They were dirty and tired and wanted nothing more than to rent quarters, eat a meal, and go to the ritual baths, not only for ritual purification in preparation for the sacrifice but also for refreshment. They often had currency not in use in Jerusalem and thus had to change money before paying for services. They preferred to use the moneychangers who had stalls within the Temple walls rather than outside because the Temple officials supervised them according to the commercial laws of Judaism and one could expect to be treated more fairly.

They stood in a moneychanger's line, dirty, and hungry, with impatient wife and children waiting. The line moved slowly. Every transaction required argument and negotiation. Sometimes, one moneychanger had to ask a colleague about an unfamiliar currency. He had to weigh the currencies, check the purity of the gold or silver. Time bore heavily. Thousands of pilgrims waited in dozens of lines. Suddenly, a strange individual appeared and turned over the tables. Mayhem ensued. The moneychangers, legitimate businessmen performing a *necessary* service, saw their wealth rolling on the ground, the tired pilgrims and their families were dismayed, and all were furious.

In the meantime, the townspeople who had prepared every spare corner of room and courtyard to rent to the pilgrims stood and waited and wondered why so few had appeared to rent space. Suddenly, they saw furious groups of pilgrims heading to the outskirts of the city to sleep in the open. They were informed that somebody named Jesus overturned the tables of the moneychangers. Many pilgrims yelled that this was the last time they were coming on pilgrimage. The stomachs of the residents sank in despair; they saw their present and perhaps future incomes disappear. The story would surely spread throughout the Jewish world. The ire of the Temple officials, of the moneychangers, of the residents, and of the pilgrims was great.

How does this story look now? Would one want to use it metaphorically to justify an action? We Jews must examine such issues to clarify our *essential* differences with Christianity.

JEWISH "LEGALISM" AND "PAROCHIALISM"

Christianity, since its inception, has presented itself as a religion based on love, in opposition to the dry formalistic legalism of the Jews. The technical term for the extreme expression of this belief is *antinomianism*. The literal meaning of which is "against the law" and, as defined by the Random House Dictionary, "maintains that Christians are freed from the moral law by virtue of grace as set forth in the gospel."

Mainstream Catholicism and Protestantism have resisted extreme conclusions regarding this radical interpretation of grace over works doctrine. But antinomians can justify their position by appealing to sources as authoritative and varied as Saint Paul, Saint Augustine, and Martin Luther.

Antinomianism runs like a thread throughout Christian history. Even today, some fundamentalists claim that because they have already been saved they no longer have any fear of hell no matter what misdemeanors and sins they might commit in the future. This is not the dominant view, but its very existence in modern Christian discourse demonstrates the residual power of antinomianism.

Why, if antinomianism has such a rich Christian pedigree, is it so severely attacked by Christian churches and theologians? Because to live in human society human beings need laws to govern their behavior. Therefore, the early Church quickly began to create a body of canon law to govern the behavior of men while on earth. Later, Calvin wrote his authoritarian *Institutes* (which indirectly molded the mentality that enabled the Salem Witch Trials). Ironically, *antinomian* Christian law is often less tolerant and less loving than "legalistic" Jewish law, perhaps because in Christian law, loss of God's grace, not sin against another human being, is the primary transgression (see *Epistle to the Romans*). Loss of God's grace is much more terrifying for the Christian than crimes against men, no matter how horrible.

A useful joint project for Jews and Christians might be to compare Canon Law as well as the laws of other Christian denominations with Jewish law in terms of its tolerance and liberalism and compare the actual behavior of each community based on Christian love and Jewish law. A one-on-one comparison on many issues might dispel the myth of loving Christianity versus a dry, legalistic Judaism. Christians require the law just as much as Jews, and Jews are instructed to act with love just as much as Christians. Dispelling these historical stereotypes might benefit both traditions. It would certainly provide a sounder foundation for a healthier Christian-Jewish dialogue.

In regards to universal Christianity versus tribal Judaism, we might compare the Christian approach regarding Jesus' monopoly power over the world to come with the Jewish approach of the *Seven Laws of Noah*, and which is better geared to living a civilized life in a pluralistic democracy.

FUTURE RULES OF JEWISH-CHRISTIAN RELATIONS: *DERECH ERETZ*

The relationship between Christians and Jews requires a new set of rules. We Jews must take the lead in setting them. Our principles must be firm, but our strategy and tactics must be informed with the principle of *Derech Eretz* – good manners. We have a dilemma. We cannot afford to offend our strongest supporters, yet we cannot avoid letting them know how much their proselytizing activities offend us when these are packaged in the *Jews for Jesus* or *Messianic Jews* packages. The majority of decent Christians will understand our position and limit these activities; for those who do not, only internal Jewish education will suffice.

We must not chastise the Christians for trying to convert us, as long as they do this openly and honestly and not under a Jewish guise. They do this with everyone, even other Christians. The late Pope had called for a Catholic counterattack against evangelical Christian inroads into traditional Catholic communities (especially in Latin America).

It is a Jewish responsibility to make Judaism stronger and more attractive by clarifying its basic principles. We must be proactive in publicizing differences between Christianity and Judaism. In a constitutional democracy that protects the citizen against religious coercion the success of missionary activity is dependent on Jewish ignorance. We are now paying the price for years of shallow and kitschy Fiddler-on-the-Roof Judaism, and the cultivation of colorful ethnicity. This must be replaced by uncompromising clarity.

We might create a Jewish organization to address the above issues. We might create a series of lectures, seminars and workshops to discuss differences between Judaism and Christianity using the books of Trude Weiss Rosmarin (*Judaism and Christianity: the Differences,* Jonathan David, 1997), Abba Hillel Silver (*Where Judaism Differed,* MacMillan, 1979), and Rudolf Augstein (*Jesus Son of Man*). This would teach Jews about their own Judaism as well as specifically clarify ideological differences between various Jewish trends. It would also be more productive for instilling Jewish ambitions than distributing "modern" graphically attractive but intellectually dishonest translations of prayer books or sustaining the bar mitzvah factory of afternoon Hebrew schools.

An advanced series of lectures, seminars, and workshops might deal with *Talmudic Thinking* versus *New Testament Thinking*. Here, we would be tactically wise to depend largely on non-Jewish sources such as Augstein's book. We might invite Christian thinkers to co-sponsor seminars with this subject as a title.

Other activities would include books, booklets, mailings, and websites that relate specifically to issues mentioned in this chapter, as well as others. We could also cultivate university debates, and television and radio talk show appearances. We could have a response team of professionals and lay people that would insist that print and electronic media clarify their meaning when using phrases such as "Talmudic thinking" or "driving out the money changers" in a pejorative way. We might develop a series of cartoons, videos, and children's books on these and other subjects. University students should have special projects that supply them with material and talking points when confronted with the subliminal anti-Jewish prejudices of western culture.

All of this can be carried out in a spirit of cooperation, good manners, and good feelings with the Christian community. It must be accompanied by the fashioning of action-oriented projects that reflect our truly shared values as well as the long-term vital interests of both communities.

CHAPTER 8

THE FUTURE OF ISRAELI CULTURE

Since Israel is the showcase of world Jewry, its internal cultural developments are of concern to *all* Jews. Israel's impact on Diaspora Jewish culture since the establishment of the State cannot be exaggerated. The most obvious example is Ashkenazi synagogues that have followed the example of Israel in using Sephardic pronunciation.

Israel is not only the largest Jewish community in the world it is also the largest Sephardic community in the world. Intermarriage between various Jewish ethnic groups is now probably over 50%, particularly in urban centers, and this has also had a great impact on Israeli and Diaspora culture. Israeli and Diaspora culture are becoming less and less distinct. Cultural fusions abound in Israel and radiate out to the Diaspora. Israel has become a leading cultural force in Diaspora Jewish life. This makes the question of the ethnic-social gap in Israel an all-Jewish problem, and Israeli cultural developments of all-Jewish significance.

PSYCHOLOGY OR SOCIOLOGY

Israel's ethnic problem is as much psychological as sociological. It stems from culture shock, cultural dismemberment, and a resultant poor self-image. An Israeli doctor of Iraqi origin, interviewed on Israeli television, explained why he left Israel and came to the United States: "In New York, I am a Jew, in Israel I am an Iraqi." This is a significant statement. For many of us, the way society views us has a lot to do with the way we view ourselves. We tend to internalize the impressions others have of us and develop characteristics others expect of us.

The great American Black leader Roy Wilkins once said, "It doesn't bother me that the Whites think we are inferior, it bothers me that *we* think we are inferior." In other words, the African-American internalized the view White America had of him; developed characteristics expected of him and began to view himself as he was viewed. The situation of the Iraqi Jewish doctor was similar. Jews as Jews may be disliked and even hated, but Gentile society sees them as intelligent and inclined to success. They are expected to be intelligent and successful. The Jews have internalized this expectation, and this might be one reason why Jews have been relatively successful. Oriental Jews in Israel, on the other hand, were expected to be backward, were treated that way, and consequently many began to behave as if it were their natural lot to be backward.

Israeli politicians and Zionist functionaries have been fond of quoting statistics showing how the standard of living of Oriental Jews has risen since their arrival in Israel. In regard to health care, nutrition, education, and housing, they are for the most part correct, but in stressing the material aspect, they miss the point. From the psychological perspective, Oriental Jewry's standard of living had often gone down.

In their countries of origin, Oriental Jews were members of the middle classes. They had a defined place in society and performed necessary tasks. They had their own culture and judged themselves by the criteria of that culture. They might have been second-class citizens and certainly suffered discrimination, but they were still subjects in control and not objects being controlled.

As many Israeli social commentators have noted, Oriental Jewish immigrants were often treated as objects. They became overwhelmed by the confusion of their new society. They felt powerless and became passive and dependent. One researcher reported that when describing their journey to Israel Oriental Jews would use the active voice – what they did. Yet when describing their experiences in Israel, they would use the passive voice – what was done to them.

CULTURE SHOCK

Substantial academic research identifies culture shock as a partial explanation for failure. One famous research project compared several hundred cases of sets of North African Jewish brothers – one who went to Israel and one who went to France. In almost every case, the French brother had been more *materially* successful. We may speculate about possible reasons. During colonial rule, the French co-opted many North African Jews into French culture. Many North African Jews became French citizens and were instrumental in spreading French culture in North Africa.

When North African Jews said they came from Southern France, it was not because they were ashamed of their origins, but because it reflected a certain reality. Numerous North African Jews were in varying degrees already French. For example France viewed Algeria as part of southern France and administered it as such. Morocco and Tunisia had a different status but many Jews there saw themselves as French. When many North African Jews moved to France, it was as if they were moving to a different area in the same country. The language, customs, bureaucracy, educational system, social mores, economy, and mentality were already familiar to them.

They arrived just as France was entering a period of sustained economic growth and becoming a consumer and service-oriented society. Thus, the lower middle class and middle class North African Jews could maintain familiar economic habits. Like their Ashkenazi brethren a century earlier, the North African Jewish middle class maintained their traditional occupations with undemanding upgrades. By performing the mercantile and service tasks they had always performed, they rapidly established a solid economic foundation in France. Being Jews, they were disliked, but by virtue of being Jews, they were expected to be educated and successful. Thus, their self-image was preserved and even enhanced.

In comparison, North African immigrants to Israel confronted an unfamiliar variation of European culture, with a mentality, life style, and expectations foreign to them. The only unifying force was their Jewishness. Israel possessed an undeveloped non-consumer economy whose mercantile sectors were already overcrowded with the Ashkenazi middle class. This obliged many North African Jews to adjust to manual labor in industry, agriculture, and lower level services. But Oriental Jews would often boast that they had never had to do physical work in their countries of origin. This cultural antipathy to physical work caused great stress. Contrast this social attitude to the fact that more than 34% of Oriental Jews in Israel had menial jobs (janitors, semi-skilled laborers, and such) as opposed to 12% of the Ashkenazi Jews, and one can comprehend the sense of fall from station.

Certain aspects of European romanticism that glorified physical work influenced the European founding fathers of Zionism. Tolstoy and his Zionist disciple, A. D. Gordon, had a great impact on the early Zionist worldview and contributed to the creation of the Jewish peasant/worker myth. The Oriental Jews had no parallel myth regarding the glories of physical labor. Oriental Jews underwent a complete change in lifestyle in a society that they did not understand. And unlike their brethren in France, they were seen as primitive and backward Asiatics who needed to be raised to the level of European civilization.

Being labeled as objectively incapable of raising themselves, the task fell to "humanitarian" and socialist Ashkenazis, who were only too glad to demonstrate their altruistic social values and humanitarianism by exposing these "unfortunates" to the glories of Western civilization. The Ashkenazi pioneers perhaps had a subconscious motivation to exaggerate Oriental Jewry backwardness as they needed to justify their own active "humanitarian" part in overcoming it. In their genuine desire to help, they destroyed the most valuable possession any individual possesses – self-respect. Viewed as welfare cases, Oriental Jews often became welfare cases.

The breakdown of the Oriental family caused by the trauma of interacting with Western culture also caused many problems. The more modern but still unprepared son became head of family, while the traditional father was relegated to a secondary and humiliating status. The father might try to exercise influence without possessing real authority, and the son would give superficial, ceremonial respect to his father while circumstance forced him to guide his father like a child. Is it any wonder that such families had such a difficult time competing in Israel, or that resentment was generated?

Despite all this, most non-Ashkenazi Jews no longer fit the above stereotypes. Perhaps only 20% of Oriental Jews can still be defined as hard-core poor. Most have raised themselves to middle-class status, in the face of tremendous odds, through sheer hard work and initiative.

ON TRADITION AND MODERNITY

The problem is not one of East versus West, but of traditional versus modern. The breakdown of tradition among Oriental Jews in Israel had also occurred among European Jews a century earlier with the spread of technology and science. In America, especially, the breakdown of traditions occurred at an astonishing rate.

Those Jews who adapted to the new society progressed. Some ultra-Orthodox communities failed to adapt. They did not progress to the same degree and remained in the ghettoes of *Bnei Brak* and Williamsburg. The poverty of Ashkenazim in *Mea Shearim* was no less than that of *Musrara*, the former North African Jerusalem slum. But the Ashkenazim managed to keep their traditional social forms intact while the Orientals did not. A major reason for this was Ashkenazi domination over religious institutions in Israel until the advent of the *Shas* Party. Thus, even the security of their own traditions was closed to the Oriental Jew, dependent as these traditions were on religious forms and expressions. The tremendous success of *Shas* bears witness to the residual need of many Oriental Jews for an authentic Oriental cultural expression with the power to compel attention and respect.

We should avoid being overly romantic and recognize that the breaking down of traditional culture is a necessary phenomenon. Traditional cultures are more than esthetic expressions of dance, song, and dress. These by themselves are simply folklore. A culture is more inclusive and extensive. It is a mindset, a mentality, and a way of looking at the world. Traditional cultures, eastern or western, are always inadequate to the needs of a dynamic technological society. The romantics who try to preserve them end up losing them in any case, with only poverty remaining.

The West modernized first, since modernity is a natural outgrowth of the internal developments of western culture. Modernity and westernization overlap. For most Third World countries, modernization and westernization is one and the same thing. This is culturally unpalatable, and sometimes the Third World vomits up its westernization, as in recent convulsions shaking the Moslem world.

IDENTITY AND RHYTHMS OF PROGRESS

The rhythm of modern society at the time a traditional culture encounters it has a lot to do with the ability of that culture to integrate. When the Ashkenazim confronted modern society, both the rhythms and standards of that society were much lower than when the Orientals encountered it. Also, the West was still largely traditional and much less secular than today. The economic opportunities of a still primitive economic system that made few demands on technical skills but responded well to energy and initiative were also an advantage.

The masses of East European Jews were just as "primitive" when they came to America as were the Orientals when they came to Israel, yet conditions in the West allowed them to make rapid economic progress. Orientals, on the other hand, encountered modern society when its rhythms and sophistication were light years ahead and when respect for tradition had all but vanished. We can liken this to jumping onto a moving train just as it is leaving the station or trying to jump on the same train as it roars through the station at 150 miles an hour.

CULTURAL ATTITUDES

The value of a culture must be judged empirically, in relation to both its adherents and to the human community in general. Every culture is of intrinsic value to those who belong to it, but this does not make it of equal value to those who do not. Mongolian culture is as significant for a Mongolian as Chinese culture is for a Chinese. Libyan culture is as significant for a Libyan as Egyptian culture is to an Egyptian. Afghani culture is as significant for an Afghani as Indian culture is to an Indian. Estonian culture is as significant for an Estonian as German culture is for a German. But to a non-member of any of these cultures Chinese, Egyptian, Indian and German cultures are of essential importance, while Mongolian, Libyan, Afghani and Estonian cultures are but marginally significant, if at all. We may say, in this context, cultural pluralism yes, multiculturalism no. Every group has the right to celebrate its own culture. This does not mean that every culture has the same *universal* value.

Many aspects of Oriental society are unacceptable to modern individuals. Attitudes toward women and some perceptions of honor have no place in modern society, and we should not even pretend to tolerate them. To accept the intrinsic value of all cultures for their adherents and to respect that fact is by no means the same as turning into a fawning white liberal, enthusing over every aspect of the exotic no matter how grotesque.

Different cultural attitudes affected perceptions of the Land of Israel itself. Oriental Jewish Zionism was essentially Biblical and messianic with only a thin overlay of modern Zionism. Many Oriental Jews came to Israel, the Holy Land, and expected to live a biblical lifestyle. They did not anticipate the technologically hyperactive society that Israel had already become. Some saw their immigration to Israel as part of the advent of the messianic period. Israel was pictured as the Garden of Eden in which God would provide and no one would have to work. Imagine the trauma of seeing the land as it was, living in refugee hovels, and being asked to do the most menial work. During the short time of a plane ride, they descended from the highest messianic expectations to the lowest reality. The better informed Ashkenazi immigrants were more pragmatic in their approach and did not suffer the cultural and psychological dislocation of their Oriental brethren.

HISTORICAL ANALOGIES

Cross-border cultural fusions have been at the root of material progress and political vigor throughout history. Cultural pluralism and openness is a prerequisite for material progress and prosperity. If Israeli culture is to have a future it must be open to outside influences and nurture pluralism. All great cultures have had this characteristic.

The so-called Golden Age of Islam was a 300-year period when Islam was a cultural crossroads, open to all the major cultures of the world from East and West. Islamic culture took the Greco-Roman tradition, by way of Byzantium and Alexandria, as well as the Persian, Chinese and Indian cultures of the day. The Arabs built on Hindu mathematics to create algebra and algorithms, as they built on Greek geometry to create the elegance of Islamic architecture.

When the Arabs turned their backs on the world following the Mongol sack of Baghdad (1258) which ended the *Caliphate* and their final "triumph" over the Crusaders (1291) their scientific and cultural progress stalled. Conversely, the "defeated" Crusaders, and the international trade that followed their misadventure, opened Europe to outside cultural influence. They brought back to Europe Arab mathematics and the Greek philosophical/scientific tradition, which the Arabs had preserved. The latter was a major contribution to the rebirth of classical humanism which resulted in the Renaissance.

Arab mathematics represented a reintroduction of quantitative forms of thought into Europe, a necessary step toward the Scientific Revolution. Copernicus, Galileo, Bacon, Descartes, and Newton would not have made their contributions to civilization had it not been for the Arab intellectual tradition. Consider the fate of Western civilization had it decided to be culturally pure and reject all foreign influences.

Europe took the compass, gunpowder, and iron foundering from the Chinese and combined them with the Arab inheritance to create a social, cultural, economic, political force that began to conquer the world. The conquest of the Americas and parts of Africa generated a tremendous surplus of gold and silver that indirectly contributed to the rise of modern investment banking as well as commercial projects to invest in. Conquering the New World introduced new agricultural products such as corn and potatoes, which resulted in population growth and expanded commodity trading in Europe.

Holland, a former Spanish colony, became the commercial and cultural crossroads of Europe. The ethnically and ideologically neutral nature of commerce made Holland a refuge for Jews and intellectuals persecuted elsewhere and helped Holland become the wealthiest and most civilized country in Europe.

Spain, on the other hand, went in the opposite direction. It instituted the Inquisition and threw out first the Jews, gutting commercial activity, and then the Moslem Moors, gutting agricultural activity. The reduction of commercial activity eventually led to a massive flight of American silver and gold bullion from Spain to Holland in the form of investments. No real investment institutions and opportunities remained in Catholic Spain. As a consequence Spain did not have a real Renaissance or Enlightenment and thus had a weaker mercantile system than France and England. Indeed, they experienced an anti-Enlightenment. In the context of European civilization, the Spanish became a "nation that dwelt alone". They turned their backs on the global developments their own exploration policy had helped to bring about and suffered the consequences.

Only in the past thirty years has Spain begun to recover from its centuries of backwardness, while Holland has been one of the most civilized countries in the world. We can see parallels to this in our own time. Saudi Arabia's tremendous oil wealth has enabled it, for a time, to turn its back on world development and norms and reinforce its medieval social structure, as did Spain 500 years ago. Saudi Arabia has been ruled by a theocratic monarchy that ignores modern standards of civil rights (especially of women). It is suspicious of foreign influences and does not engage in real industrial, agricultural, and commercial development because it has always had oil to fall back on, just as Spain depended on its bullion. As with Spain, this is beginning to have disastrous economic and social consequences for the Saudi people. Saudi per capita income has been halved in the past two decades. Like Spain, Saudi Arabia has been exporting its capital in the search for investment opportunities unavailable at home. Like Spain, Saudi Arabia has moved from tremendous currency reserves to tremendous foreign debt. To offset this, they must open their economy and their culture. They must reform their entire political system and like it or not, become more western. Like pre-20th century Spain, they appear unable or unwilling to do this in any significant way.

England's economy benefited greatly when it gave refuge to Protestant Huguenot craftsmen fleeing French persecution. Likewise, when Idi Amin expelled thousands of Indian merchants and professionals, their loss was a major factor in Uganda's thirty years of subsequent economic decline. In England, however, these refugees have made an impressive economic contribution. We see the same lack of wisdom almost repeated in Fiji, where indigenous Fijians wanted to toss out the Indian business class. If they had succeeded, Fiji would have been set back fifty years. The intertwining of cultural openness and economic development is self-evident throughout history.

Racism and discrimination are a sure formula for backwardness. Just look at the American South before the success of the civil rights movement. The liberation of southern Blacks from the yoke of Jim Crow helped integrate the South into America's continental economy and accelerated its economic growth. Paradoxically, this benefited the southern White even more than it did the southern Black.

The United States is the quintessential open society whose entire economic, commercial, scientific, and technological history is based on vast migrations of peoples of different cultures. One of the reasons for the backwardness of the South relative to the North prior to the Civil Rights Movement was the lack of immigration to that area and the consequent lack of the cultural diversity that is a stimulus to creativity. The United States became the scientific capital of the world as a consequence of the Nazi conquest of Europe. The European scientists and engineers who flooded into the United States before and following World War II culminated a historical process dependent upon the inventiveness and energy of immigrants. From Scottish steel maker Andrew Carnegie to Swiss chemist Pierre Dupont to German inventor Charles Steinmetz (the wizard of Westinghouse) to the Jew Albert Einstein to the Italian Enrico Fermi, America's material and moral progress has relied on an open society.

Consider that while the United States opened itself to the world and to immigrants, the Soviet Union closed itself off from the world and developed a xenophobia that put tens of thousands of foreign residents into forced labor camps. This self-inflicted cultural claustrophobia drove much of their own scientific and cultural talent to look for ways to escape to the West.

THE CULTURAL HISTORY OF ISRAEL

Israel's cultural history has developed in a different direction. The pioneering stage was insular and suspicious of outside influences. When I arrived in Israel in the late 1960s, Israel's cultural menu consisted of classical music and what is called "Land of Israel" music, (much of which actually derived from Russian and Ukrainian folk music).

All other music was held suspect by the political and cultural establishment. "Salon music" (popular dance music) was thought to signify cultural decadence. How would a generation raised on something so superficial be able to fight and defend the country? The adverse attitudes toward popular Western culture were so extreme that the Israeli government dedicated several sessions to debate the question of entrance visas for the *Beatles*. The visa request was eventually denied in order to protect the youth from their destructive influence. The extraordinary achievements of the salon-music generation during the Six-Day War dispelled such silly notions. In hindsight, the Six-Day War and its political and economic aftermath may have been the turning point as Israel developed a much more open, self-confident, and pluralistic culture.

This provincial cultural attitude was particularly apparent in regards to middle eastern music. Up until the 1980s, this music was denigrated as "cassette music" because it was usually self-recorded on cheap radio-tape cassettes because the major Israeli record companies would not record such culturally inferior fare. Another term was "Central Bus Station" music, because the Oriental music cassette shops were mostly located at the Tel Aviv Central Bus Station. Oriental Jewish music was granted one or two hours a day on the Israeli radio and was always defined as folk music. Once a year, an Oriental Jewish Music festival and contest appeared on television. This was as far as the cultural/media establishment of Israel was prepared to go in recognizing the cultural legitimacy of more than 50% of Israel's Jewish population. Arabic music was totally taboo and limited to the Arabic language broadcasts only.

The enforcement of these cultural norms was fierce. As a volunteer on a kibbutz after the Six-Day War, I once turned on a radio station transmitting Arabic music. I thought that in order to understand the Middle East I should at least make an attempt to understand its culture. A young kibbutznik walked into my room and angrily turned off my radio: "We do not listen to such garbage here." Later, a female volunteer tried to enter the dining room wearing a beautiful Arab dress. She was denied entrance because she was inappropriately dressed. Both of these events occurred on a progressive, peace-loving, workers-of-the-world-unite kibbutz – the ultimate reverie of the Left. Ironically, the Israeli Right was much more tolerant of Oriental Jewish culture as the Oriental Jews were their natural political constituency.

To be fair, these attitudes quickly changed in the six years between the Six-Day and Yom Kippur wars. In the early 1970s, Israeli women were in fashion if they wore Bedouin dresses, and Israeli fashion in general adapted many Middle Eastern motifs. The official keepers of the Israeli cultural gate, however, discriminated against Oriental music until the 1990s. Today, thankfully, it is part of the Israeli cultural mainstream, and Oriental musical motifs have become an integral part of mainstream Israeli popular music.

Before the Six-Day War, Israel was culturally provincial, and its knowledge based exports totaled about 17 million dollars a year. Today, Israel's cultural menu is probably one of the most diverse in the world, and its knowledge based exports total more than 30 billion dollars a year. Innovation is a cultural characteristic and cultural openness and technological innovation are two sides of the same coin. Because of this Israel has become an interesting cultural and technological center.

But cultural openness does not mean cultural relativity. A hierarchy of cultural values exists and there must be a meta-cultural foundation. In the United States, the meta-cultural foundation is the Constitution, a set of basic values to which all subcultures declare loyalty. There is a profound difference between cultural pluralism and multiculturalism.

THE FUTURE

All this is past tense. The question remains, what will be the future of Israeli society? Will it be demographically Oriental and culturally Western, or will Israel emulate the United States and constantly create and recreate its cultural life while paying scant attention to the sources of its cultural raw material? Do American musicians really care if their cultural raw materials are Scots-Irish, African, or Latin?

Musically, at least, the future is now. Current Israeli music is already a mixture of classical East and West, modern pop and ethnic. One can hear music in Hebrew with Latin and Arabic motifs wrapped in the driving beat of modern pop. Mixtures such as these will continue to develop, driven by a combination of technology, communications, and cross-border migrations of peoples carrying different cultural baggage. It is interesting to note that countries or regions with the highest percentage of immigrants are the most technologically and culturally dynamic. Technological progress is a cultural attribute and a consequence of cultural openness and pluralism. This has given Israel its qualitative edge over its enemies. Any attempt to make Israeli culture mono-dimensional will have serious negative consequences.

As noted, cultural pluralism suggests that the richer and more varied the cultural mix, the healthier the cultural ecology will be. Healthy cultural ecologies produce economic and technological dynamism because they introduce a multiplicity of viewpoints into the creative mix. In this sense, cultural diversity is a vital survival tool for humanity. With it, we can adapt to economic and technological environments now changing in real time: the greater the number of viewpoints, the greater the chance that someone will come up with the solution for a vital problem.

Individuals who cultivate *within themselves* a plurality of cultures also have a much better chance of succeeding. For example, I am

Jewish, American, Ashkenazi, Israeli, Middle Eastern, European, and a world citizen. I am all these at once. Such should be the attitude of cultural discourse in Israel and the Diaspora in the 21st century. This would be a healthy model for all residents of the planet in the 21st century. To the extent that Israel and the Jewish people at large can make this cultural attitude a norm, we will truly be a *light unto the nations*.

Multiculturalism is contrary to the above. It says there are no objective cultural values, that values are subjective constructs. In this view, to speak of values in terms of some objective moral and ethical standard is foolish and misleading. All values are subjective, and culture is an ideology that reflects these subjective values. There is, therefore, no hierarchy of cultural values. All cultures are created equal and should be treated as equal. Multiculturalists see rationalism as a Western ideology, not an objectively consistent value. Non-rational societies and cultures are equal to rational societies and culture; rationality has no prerogative over irrationality; there is no objective thought, only subjective feeling.

Taken to its extreme, a consistent multi-culturalist would deny the *Universal Declaration of Human Rights* because there is no such thing as a universal concept of human rights, and therefore the universal declaration must be cultural imperialism. I have been told that some anthropologists have already made this claim. The rights stated in the *Declaration* are based on the values of western civilization as they matured during the European Enlightenment. These include the sanctity and primacy of the individual, possessing certain natural inalienable rights by the very fact of being a human being.

The former prime ministers of Singapore and Malaysia have denigrated this "western ideology" and raised the flag of "Asian values." This vague term celebrates the collective over the individual and the wisdom of the patriarchal leader over the judgment of the individual citizen. It is designed to justify authoritarian rule.

This debate is especially relevant for Israel, as the Arabs have constantly claimed that Israel is a foreign western implant and should integrate itself into the region, that is, reject the West and integrate itself into the Middle East. Let us examine this claim in greater detail. When we get specific, we can easily see the absurdities of multiculturalism as it applies to Israel's future.

Should Israel aspire to the judicial system of Iran or the judicial system of England?

Should Israel aspire to the civil service of Egypt or the civil service of France?

Should Israel aspire to the rights of women in Saudi Arabia or the rights of women in Sweden?

Should Israel aspire to the technological level of Yemen or the technological level of the United States?

Should Israel aspire to a Third World standard of living or to a Western standard of living?

Should Israel aspire to a welfare society or to a subsistence society?

There is a hierarchy of values. A culture that implements the death penalty is inferior to that which has rejected the death penalty. A culture that cuts off the hands of thieves is inferior to a culture that imprisons them. A culture that places the state above the individual is inferior to a culture that places the individual above the state. A culture that denies women equal rights is inferior to a culture that recognizes that women are inherently equal. A culture that stresses the past is inferior to a culture that stresses the future. A culture intolerant of criticism is inferior to a culture that encourages criticism.

So, what is the future of Israeli culture? *Cultural pluralism yes, multiculturalism, no!* We must strive to create a meta-culture that is "western," that reflects the principles of the *Universal Declaration of Human Rights* and contains subcultures that do not contradict these basic western meta-cultural values. We should cultivate a proliferation of esthetic cultural expressions that draw their raw material from every culture on the planet but remain anchored in western concepts of rights and social and economic organization. We must be constantly inspired by the variegated cultural traditions of the Jews as we have developed over the past 4,000 years and as we will continue to develop into the future.

A cultural vision based upon reconstructing past cultural achievements is a prescription for ruin. *We live in the future and not in the past.* We require a future-oriented Jewish cultural attitude that will cultivate romantic yearnings for the future instead of obsolete yearnings for the past.

| CHAPTER 9 |

WHY BE JEWISH?

A growing number of non-orthodox Israelis and Diaspora Jews have difficulty answering this question. This is the question of questions. Unless we provide a social and cultural framework in which the majority of non-orthodox Jews can provide themselves with a satisfactory answer, the issue of any Jewish future will be moot. The Jews are perhaps the only people who would even ask such a question. This in itself is one of the characteristics of Jewish uniqueness.

However, the dilemma of identity is not unique to the Jews. *The challenge facing all cultures in the 21st century is how to assimilate into the modern world without being assimilated into it.* Identity has become more a matter of individual choice than of historical inheritance. Individuals today pick and choose from various cultural sources that are valuable for them.

Cultural traditions are no longer "sold" as being inherently valuable. Value is argued in terms of what is beneficial for you as an individual. Spend a day or two watching the numerous televangelists and you will be struck that much of their preaching deals with how belief in Jesus helps overcome personal problems. Sermons often resemble self-improvement seminars clothed in theological garb. This is unlike earlier fire-and-brimstone, fear-of-hell sermons. In the present era cultural traditions that provide spiritual benefit for groups of individuals over periods of time will survive.

THE ADVENT OF MULTIFACETED IDENTITY

It is no longer the customs and prohibitions of the traditional inherited community that decides identity, but rather the modern individual. Identity can be multifaceted. The Jewish tradition is flexible, based as it is on personal behavior rather than doctrinal belief. It is capable of accommodating numerous cultural accretions, as long as these do not contain beliefs, practices, or dogmas that contradict Jewish tradition but only add another dimension to the Jewish individual's spiritual life.

Judaism can afford to be tolerant of the phenomenon. Imitation is not only the sincerest form of flattery it is also a test of a culture's vigor. A vigorous culture possessed of self-esteem and self-confidence will take freely from other cultures without fear of "cultural pollution" and by doing this, will add to its own vigor. A closed, fearful ghettoized culture will result in the cultural equivalent of genetic inbreeding and create cultural dullards.

This tolerance cannot stretch to include the *Jews for Jesus*. Nor are Jewish communities ever likely to accommodate the *Jews for Jesus* phenomenon, the manipulative appeal to Jewish open-mindedness notwithstanding. A comparable ideological conflict would exist with Islam. The fact that Mohammed is beyond criticism and that even implied criticism might earn one a death sentence is contrary to Judaism, a religion and culture which depicts its great biblical heroes in all their human frailties. The perception of Jesus and Mohammed as being above criticism is foreign to the Jewish mentality.

- The Bible depicts Abraham misrepresenting the marital status of Sarah to gain advantage in a real estate deal.
- Jacob cheats Esau out of his inheritance by lying to his father, Isaac.
- Jacob's sons sell their brother Joseph into slavery out of sibling jealousy.
- Moses is depicted in the sources and in popular Jewish culture as

having a severe speech defect (generating many Jewish jokes about how this caused grave misunderstandings between Moses and God.)

- David sends his best friend off to die in battle so that he can sleep with his wife.
- Solomon had a thousand wives and concubines.

Jewish heroes are not wispy, ethereal, "spiritual" beings; they are flesh-and-blood human beings with openly documented flaws. This distinguishes Judaism from other traditions that portray their heroes as being above all human frailty.

HUMAN-CENTERED IDENTITY

Judaism encourages active criticism, not passive acceptance because it has always stressed the centrality of human behavior. The Talmud says that man *must be a partner with God in the (ongoing) act of creation*. This is what obligates the humanistic Jewish concept of *Tikkun Olam* (repairing/improving the world). The primacy of individual moral autonomy appears throughout the Jewish tradition:

- Abraham argues with God over the fate of Sodom and Gomorrah.
- He interrupts a "conversation" with God to offer hospitality to three strangers.
- The Jews say, "*Derech eretz kodem leTorah*": "Proper behavior takes precedence over the Torah." In other words, your responsibility toward your fellow human beings takes precedence over your obedience to God. This is the true significance of the "Sacrifice of Isaac" story – not Abraham's obedience to God but the end of human sacrifice as a means to placating God, thereby affirming the centrality of human life.
- There is the previously mentioned Talmudic story about sages who reject the very voice of God as having weight in an argument. The rejection highlights the principle of human moral and intellectual

autonomy. The story demonstrates the principle of majority rule, minority rights and human intellectual autonomy and sovereignty, even in regards to God.

- On Yom Kippur, you request forgiveness for transgressions against God. A sin against another human being cannot be forgiven by God, but only by that person.

IDENTITY AS AN EVOLUTIONARY PROCESS

Identity is evolutionary. To be English today is different from being English in the time of Queen Victoria, Elizabeth I, or Alfred the Great. Similarly, being Jewish today is different from being Jewish a hundred years ago, five hundred years ago, or two thousand years ago.

Identity as an evolutionary process is especially applicable to the Jews. A normative, restricted definition of what it means to be Jewish is impossible. The Jews are an ideologically and culturally pluralistic people. Ideologically, Jewish identity can include ultra-Orthodox, modern Orthodox, Conservative, Reform, Reconstructionist, and Humanist Judaism. Jewish identity also includes secular atheists and agnostics such as some of the greatest Jews of the 20th century: Einstein, Freud, Ben Gurion, Jabotinsky, and others. Jewish identity includes German, Yemenite, Russian, Iraqi, Moroccan and American Jews. The only universal norms of Jewish identity are the prohibition against idolatry and the requirement of unqualified individual responsibility.

The test is empirical. If a form of Judaism endures, it is because it has contributed something of value to a critical mass of individuals. It is the spiritual equivalent of the survival of the fittest. What survives does so because it answers a need and gives value to real human beings. Culture is not preserved, it is created, and it evolves as a consequence of its dynamic interaction with other cultures and other cultural environments. What does not interact does not evolve; what does not evolve dies.

The way you behave (*Derech Eretz*) is central to Jewish tradition, not your ideological belief system. The hijacking of Jewish tradition by a politicized religious establishment presenting itself as "authentic" Judaism has alienated many Israelis and Diaspora Jews from Jewish tradition itself.

JEWISH CITIZENSHIP

In the past, a common belief system, common ethnic characteristics, or combination of both determined identity. In the future, however, Jewish identity will probably be pluralistic, based upon common norms of communal behavior and communal obligation – what I would call *Jewish citizenship*.

Concepts of citizenship stress behavior, not belief. They are, therefore, secular. In the 21st century, Jewish identity will most probably be formulated within a secular pluralistic framework. Components of Jewish identity will be religious and secular, but while religious identities have been able to flourish within secular frameworks, secular identities have not usually been able to exist within strict religious frameworks.

A secular Jewish framework based on Jewish citizenship has become a survival necessity. In the modern Diaspora, more than 50% of young Jews marry non-Jews. The Jewish and non-Jewish partners are usually nonreligious. Religious conversion is at present the only method available for the non-Jewish partner to join the Jewish people. This creates an absurd situation in which the agnostic non-Jewish partner is expected to be more observant than the agnostic Jewish partner. An agreed upon falsehood becomes the basis for membership in the Jewish community. Is it any wonder that both Jewish and non-Jewish partners increasingly refuse to partake of this spiritual mendacity?

Intermarriage is not causing assimilation, but rather the lack of nonreligious means enabling people to join the Jewish community. A concept of Jewish citizenship might provide a palatable alternative. This could reverse the demographic erosion threatening the Jewish people.

The *Society for Humanistic Judaism* might have the potential to fill this role but would have to do two things in order to do so. First, it would have to grow significantly in numbers in order to have practical impact on the community at large. Second, it would have to imbue its innovative approach to Judaism with a stress on the future. Post-Enlightenment, post-industrial urban Jewry is future-oriented in its economic, social, intellectual and even its cultural life. *Humanistic Judaism* developing new ways of celebrating Jewish holidays or the ceremonies of the Jewish life cycle is not sufficient. When this new movement becomes future oriented it will have a compelling message that will help it grow into a major Jewish phenomenon – in Israel as well as in the Diaspora.

PLURALISM VERSUS HOMOGENEITY

The Orthodox call for a clarified, homogeneous, "authentic" Jewish identity is counterproductive to Jewish survival. Heterogeneous pluralism, not homogeneous orthodoxy, is increasingly the choice of Jews.

The inability of the Jewish People to recognize pluralism as the norm of modern Jewish life has produced new "unifying" idolatries. Israel and Holocaust idolatry have replaced God as centerpieces for Jewish communal "worship." But Israel is a state, and a state is an instrument, not a holy icon to be worshipped. The Holocaust is a terrible historical event, not a philosophical basis for a new theology.

We should remember that fascism is a perverted secularization of the religious instinct that makes the nation and the state an object of worship. There is a delicate line between patriotism as a healthy love for the scenery, odors, food, and customs of one's own country and people, and a chauvinism that manifests contempt for other peoples or countries. The latter is an inevitable consequence of state and nation worship. The Jews in particular must be wary not to fall into this trap.

When we make the Holocaust the central component of Jewish identity, we risk destroying the desire of many young people to remain Jewish. They are looking for something of value for their future and most have no desire to be obsessively preoccupied with terrible past events. Respectful remembrance is historically necessary, politically wise, and spiritually healthy. But feeding young Jews a constant diet of the Holocaust as the defining mark of Jewish identity is dangerous if our primary aim is to cultivate a healthy identification with Jewish tradition and nurture aspirations for a meaningful collective Jewish future.

The pluralistic Jew may, at various times and for various reasons, utilize particular elements of tradition, but this cannot be the backbone of a future-oriented Jewish identity. Over thirty years ago, Arthur Lewis, the Black Nobel Prize winner in economics, criticized the ethnic kitsch of black cultural nationalism by writing: " . . .*only decadent peoples on the way down feel an urgent need to mythologize and live in their past. A vigorous people, on the way up, is more concerned with visions of its future.*"

Jewish identity cannot rest upon a doctrinaire interpretation of Jewish religiosity, as the Orthodox would have it. Nor can it rest upon a Jewish version of Zorba the Greek, as the early Zionist pioneers would have had it. Since the Dispersion, the Jews have developed a multiplicity of ethnicities. And since the Enlightenment, they have been the avant-garde of cosmopolitan culture.

Every Jew is at once the possessor of five cultural traditions and identities:

- the totality of Jewish history,
- a personal Jewish ethnic tradition (Ashkenazi, Sephardic, or such),
- all other Jewish ethnic traditions,
- the culture of the country they live in, and
- the cultures of all humanity.

In this mixing of various cultures the modern Jewish world citizen is no different from any other modern world citizen.

Responsible, self-confident Jews must balance these five identities into an integrated whole. This whole will be distinctive for each individual. In other words, every Jew will possess his or her own personal integrated whole of Jewish/human identity, and only a generally agreed upon system of Jewish citizenship will be capable of unifying them. This might be the key to the future of communal Jewish identity.

Jewish identity still contains some elements of a tribal identity. We often refer to ourselves as the tribe, yet we are a very a unique tribe. *We are the only tribe whose fundamental ethos is a universal vision for all humankind.* In its ideal form, the tribal is subordinate to the universal. We justify our own existence and historical role in terms of all humanity and not only in terms of ourselves. Our central national myth has to do with the universal redemption of all humankind. If we turn our backs on universal humanity, we turn our backs on ourselves, on our own tribe.

Rabbi Kook, Ashkenazi Chief Rabbi in the Land of Israel during the British Mandate, believed that the world is continually evolving toward universalism, yet because so many of our actions reflect individual nations, the universal ideal must be realized by way of enlightened nationalism. In this, he was an unknowing student of the great liberal Italian nationalist Mazzini. Kook saw Zionism as an essential step in the divine scheme of evolution toward universalism. He considered it the Jewish people's mission to devote themselves to the divine goal of human perfection and universalism. According to Kook, God imposed this task upon the Jews by choosing them, and it is up to the Jews to accept this task and fulfill this divine mission. Here, the Jewish tradition of *Tikkun Olam* and the western tradition of Utopianism meet.

THE TRANSITION GENERATION

We survive today only through the inertia of the forms that grew out of a unifying belief system and the behaviors that grew out of a common ethnicity.

We are the *transition generation*, the cultural equivalent of the *desert generation*. Many of us have an unarticulated feeling that Jewish identity is important, even though we cannot say why. This derives to a degree from the more general human need for some kind of particular identity that will be a cultural and spiritual anchor in an age of alienation. We sense that we have inherited something rich and wonderful, yet in a form that is of little spiritual use to us. We can use this instinctive feeling as a foundation upon which to build a new concept of Jewish identity.

We would be wise to follow the advice of Sumner Redstone, CEO of Viacom/CBS/Paramount, who, in a television interview, said, "*History affects the future, but it should never get in the way of the future.*" We require a fundamental reevaluation of our tradition as we review it through the prism of our modern reality.

Fundamental reevaluation obliges creative reinterpretation and does not require rejecting the valuable parts of our tradition because they are often imbedded in formulations unacceptable to the modern mind. In this context, the original intent of the sources is less important than a creative reinterpretation of them. What would be the fate of constitutional law if original intent were applied as an absolute? Would we reject the American Constitution because the founding fathers allowed slavery? Would we reject the American Declaration of Independence because it contains a racist slur against the American Indians? Would we reject the Magna Carta principle that men have property over themselves because its original intent was only for the nobility?

Human beings who have cultural self-assurance strive to extract what is valuable to the modern individual out of their cultural tradition without fearing that they are somehow traitors to their people. Human beings with self-esteem know that a tradition that does not evolve and develop becomes obsolete and eventually extinct. The claim by the modern Orthodox Rabbinate that we are obliged to accept our tradition 'whole cloth' is a threat to the continuation of Jewish culture in the global age. It also stands in opposition to the self-correcting mechanism of Jewish history that has enabled us to survive thus far.

FROM RIGHT TO EXIST TO REASON TO EXIST

It is not enough to say that the Jews have a right to exist. Of course we do. The question is: why should nonreligious Jews feel the need or perceive the value in continuing to exist as Jews? From a purely rational standpoint, this question has no answer. From a purely rational standpoint, assimilation is a perfectly legitimate alternative. This is why those of us concerned with the Jewish future must strive to make Jewishness meaningful to the modern Jew. In its present form, the question of sustaining a Jewish identity is meaningless for many young modern Jews. How do we make it meaningful?

Religious Jews "believe in God." They have an inherent sense of the unique collective mission of the Jewish people in God's service. But many Jews today do not believe in God, and most do not practice the ritual mitzvoth. Rather they sense uniqueness about themselves as products of an exceptional historical adventure and some merit in their continued Jewish existence and identity.

One can be a truly cosmopolitan Jew, yet still recognize the distinctiveness of Jewish identity and its unique contribution to civilization. The challenge today is to see how sustaining one's Jewish identity gives one spiritual and cultural value. What would it take to motivate young, university-educated Jews to invest time and energy in trying to define a meaningful Jewish identity? This is not only a question of education or propaganda. It requires a redefinition of the contents and forms of Jewish identification.

HISTORICAL CONTEXT

What are the social, cultural, and scientific conditions that frame our existence? After all, individual identity is rooted in the objective conditions that mold our cultural environment. Judaism was born and developed in the agricultural era but has hardly come to terms with the post-Enlightenment industrial reality that created modern Jewry. In short, there is a fundamental disconnection between classical Judaism and modern Jewry.

Jean Paul Sartre was once bitterly condemned by us for claiming that the Jews were a product of anti-Semitism, and not the reverse (implying that the Jews would disappear once anti-Semitism disappeared). This was, of course, a vulgar Marxist interpretation of history characteristic of a certain type of intellectual. It is certainly an inadequate and impoverished explanation for the whole of Jewish history. Yet, if we were completely honest with ourselves, we would be forced to admit that for much of the 20th century, what we call Jewish identity has been the product of or reaction to modern anti-Semitism. Certainly, Zionism and American Jewish organizational life are impossible to understand or explain except in this context.

Modern Jewish life is almost entirely a reaction to the internal developments of 19th and 20th century European civilization. Zionism, and the Reform, Conservative, neo-Orthodox, Yiddishist, and Bundist movements were reactions to vast social, political, and economic changes of another culture. In this regard, the Jews are no different from the Arabs, Chinese, Indians, or Africans. The modern history of all non-European peoples is a reaction to 19th and 20th century Europe. The Jews are unique, however, because the early stages of their reaction took place in Europe just as they were making significant contributions to and becoming part of Europe.

Some nations have reacted more successfully to westernization and modernization than others. The Japanese, Chinese, and Koreans have all accommodated the West without sacrificing their uniqueness. The Iranians and certain segments of the Moslem world have rebelled against westernization and modernization. Other segments of the Moslem world such as Turkey and Malaysia have been as successful as the Koreans in adapting.

The Jews have three options: the Japanese model, the Iranian model, or the assimilationist model. At its outset, Zionism seemed to anticipate the Japanese model, but today Israeli culture seems a battle between the Iranian and assimilationist (post-Zionist) models. This has grave consequences for the future of Israel-Diaspora relations and Diaspora Jewry.

SPIRITUAL PIONEERS

When the Jews were spiritual pioneers and creators, they were a powerful force in history, imitated by others. Jewish identity was inherently compelling. Ethical monotheism has sustained us and made us a force in human history for more than 3,000 years. The various Jewish responses to the 18th century European Enlightenment have sustained us for the past two centuries. Today, however, most Jews do not believe in a supernatural, judgmental God and the secular frameworks of the Enlightenment seem to be increasingly inadequate for the spiritual needs of humanity.

The growing perception that secular Enlightenment frameworks do not satisfy a basic human need for something "beyond" might be one of the major causes for the worldwide return to fundamentalist religiosity. The Jewish responses to the Enlightenment (Reform, Conservative, and Zionism) appear increasingly inadequate to the task of sustaining Jewish identity. For the first time in Zionist history, Orthodox Judaism is in the ascendant and secular Zionism is on the defensive. This is not a consequence of the political advantage gained by the various Orthodox trends in Israel. Rather, their political advantage is a consequence of their spiritual ascendance, garnered as a result of their satisfying the spiritual emptiness of many secular Jews.

The Orthodox see this as a validation of their belief system and proof of their eventual triumph within the Jewish world. They can now supply empirical evidence that the only real barricade against Jewish assimilation is belief, and therefore a general Jewish strategy of survival must center on belief. But few Jews can make themselves believe in what they don't believe in, even if it is "good for the Jews." The Orthodox say we must believe in order to survive, but one cannot believe in belief; one cannot believe because it is nice or psychologically healthy to believe in something, or because belief helps preserve our ethnic identity. Today, we require new Jewish expressions for the postmodern period. The Jews must strive to become spiritual pioneers of a new world civilization. The Jews have no models to copy, as they did following the Enlightenment. It is now incumbent upon us to create the model that others will copy. Our ancestors were spiritual pioneers in ancient times when they created monotheism. Present generations should strive to once again become spiritual pioneers. This could be a promise for our meaningful existence as Jews.

CHAPTER 10

TRANSFORMATION

Perennial Jewish questions are: "Who is a Jew?" and "What is Judaism?". Jews have been arguing over this since the European Enlightenment and will likely continue to do so for generations to come.

Less controversial is the feeling that being a Jew means to sense oneself as part of a community. Jewish identity and Jewish community are for many Jews one and the same. Significance of community is a fundamental value of Judaism. It is not an exaggeration to claim that alienation from the community is a greater cause of assimilation than one's lack of ritual observance or religious agreement. This is because being Jewish manifests itself in a sense of belonging and an active desire to attach oneself to some aspect of Jewish communal life no matter what one's level of religious observance.

Although it is impossible to call someone an agnostic or atheist Christian or Moslem, the phrases "he is an agnostic Jew" or "she is a Jewish atheist" are perfectly logical in a Jewish context. Judaism might be a religion, but Jewishness is an ethnicity. Yet modernity has been eroding this sense of community for the past several centuries, and globalization now presents even greater challenges to its continuation.

Judaism has survived because it has been historically adaptive. From the patriarchs through the judges and kings to the prophets, throughout the 2,000-year history of rabbinical Judaism, the Jews adapted to the necessities of mostly negative external forces. However, modern global civilization has now given us the positive opportunity to exploit our adaptive gifts for our own creative growth rather than as a response to negative externals.

Globalization has created its own antithesis, the desire of "small" peoples to maintain their cultural uniqueness. This desire is welcome and healthy, if we apply the model of ecological diversity to human culture.

GLOBALIZED ZIONISM

How can we correlate Zionism with an emerging global reality that the founders of Zionism could not have conceived? Classical Zionism saw the Land of Israel as the only place where Jews could prosper and maintain their heritage. Today, however, globalization and the affirmation of cultural pluralism are enabling various ethnic Diasporas to maintain and even enrich their cultural heritages in countries far away from their homelands.

The question of sustaining a Diaspora identity is no longer an exclusively Jewish issue. The existence and success of other Diaspora global tribes (Indians, Koreans, Chinese) is well documented in Joel Kotkin's book *Tribes* (Random House, 1994). The universal Jewish Diaspora must cease to be viewed as a disease that the Jews must be cured of (the view of classical Zionism). Instead, the Diaspora must be seen as a Jewish and Zionist resource that would have to be invented if it did not already exist.

The Internet, joined to the fact of Israel's existence as the largest Jewish community in the world, changes the very concept of aliya. We may now talk about the plausibility of *intellectual aliya*. A Jew might live in London, New York, or Los Angeles and transmit his or her intellectual product to Israel, to an Israeli company or organization operating outside of Israel, or to other Diaspora communities. Conversely a Jew would be able to work in New York or Paris or Tokyo and still reside in Tel Aviv or a kibbutz. Tom Friedman in *The World is Flat* describes numerous instances of such activities which might be replicated in a Jewish context.

In the Internet world we can envision a multitude of Jewish cultural centers, numerous cultural nodes existing on a global Jewish cultural network, reflecting the rich cultural pluralism that characterizes every Jewish community in the world today. The future may consist of 50 Israeli nodes, 20 North American Jewish nodes, and 15 European Jewish nodes as well as other cultural nodes in Latin America, Australia etc.

Rather than one Israeli-Diaspora relationship, we might have a multitude of Israeli-Diaspora relationships, as well as Diaspora-Diaspora relationships and Israeli-Israeli relationships. If we look at current reality as it is rather than through ideological blinders, we would recognize that such relationships already exist because World Jewry constitutes a multifaceted world community.

SYNERGY AND THE JEWISH QUESTION

Synergy refers to effective mutually beneficial cooperation. The Jews face a cultural and communal choice, either to prosper by striving for cultural synergy between Jewish and global culture or to decline. History records examples of synergies that have created new cultural patterns which advanced both cultures to a higher stage of creativity. Synergy has always been a key element in Jewish history. In the 21st century we are faced with the challenge of cultivating synergy between global and Jewish cultures.

Jews have lived in Babylon, Egypt, Canaan, Greece, Rome, Medieval Christendom, the Islamic Caliphate, Modern Europe, and

North America. These experiences were synergetic. These cultures contributed to and transformed the Jews, and the Jews in turn contributed to them. The most striking example of this synergy is the American Jewish experience.

By adopting a strategy of synergy, we are obliged to do away with the notion that the history of the Jews is only one of suffering and persecution. It is time to reject this woeful premise of Jewish history. Many peoples have suffered terribly in human history, the Jews included, but neither human history nor Jewish history is simply the story of suffering.

The recognition that Jewish history has not been one long unique tragedy is not to discount the uniqueness of the Nazi Holocaust. But the Czarist "Pale of Settlement" has its parallel in apartheid South Africa and Jews being limited to certain trades has its parallels in the *Eta* of Japan and the *Untouchables* of India. Pogroms, massacres, and lynching are a universal and not a uniquely Jewish phenomenon. The histories of the Armenians, Tutsis, and American Blacks confirm this.

Jewish hand-wringing is a hazard to our well being. How can it not alienate increasing numbers of young Jews? *What mentally healthy person wants to be part of a culture that is dedicated to never-ending mourning, let alone devote his or her life to that culture?* We need a positive vision of a creative Jewish future based on the positive aspects of our history. The Jews have been contributors to every civilization they have lived in; shaped by and shaping them. This must continue to be the case as we contribute to the creation of a new human civilization that will also change us.

The second stage of the Jewish liberation movement called Zionism must be a self-emancipation from our own self-pity. We Jews must change our outlook. Of course we must respect our past, honor our heritage, and pay tribute to the majestic achievements of previous generations. But, most of all, we must look forward into the future, to actualizing ourselves in and contributing to the world of the 21st century.

INDIVIDUALISM AND COMMUNITY

The rise of individualism does not necessitate a breakdown of community. We should change our mode of thinking from breakdown to transformation. Communal frameworks should be designed to reflect and foster the individual Jew's search for meaning. This would be a new kind of social contract, whereby the individual's responsibility to the community depends on the community providing space for individual actualization.

We can only sustain community by recognizing and celebrating individualism. Cultures that repress individualism cannot flourish in a world characterized by rapid rates of change. Moralistic preaching about communal responsibility that negates self-concern is likely to alienate young Jews and prove that Jewish communal involvement is not relevant to their lives.

The unifying theme of the 21st century is the significance of the individual. This is as much a doctrine of individual responsibility as of individual self-realization. Not the self-indulgence of the "me" generation, but a new ethical concept that elevates individual responsibility to a global level and recognizes that individual efforts matter and are central to social morality.

This is reflected in classical Jewish sources. Hillel begins with the individual: *"If I am not for myself, who will be for me?"* He recognizes, however, that without society, individual existence is essentially meaningless when he continues: *"If I am only for myself, what am I?"* Hillel goes on to recognize the significance of time in the individual/ society equation when he queries, *"If not now, when?"* Can any quotation in the history of culture have anticipated the needs of the real-time change inherent to globalization so succinctly?

Hillel addresses the centrality of the individual, the necessity of society, and the requirements of time. When individuals act "in time" for themselves and society, they sanctify. The Jews can now sanctify the mundane by actualizing themselves, each component – individual, society, and time – serving the other.

Another Jewish source says *"Bishvili Nivrah Haolam"*, ("for my sake the world was created"). This means that "I" am the aim and the purpose of creation and my existence is its own justification. It also means that I am responsible for this world, else I will not exist.

CUSTOMIZATION AND COMMUNITY

The Jewish experience must be customized to the needs of the individual Jew. Platonic abstractions such as the "Jewish people" will be meaningless unless they are directed to the real needs of real Jewish persons. What type of Jewish community will help the Jewish person realize his or her individuality? Jewish identity and Israel will continue to have diminishing relevance for the Internet generation unless both provide individual lives with meaning and an outlet for creativity.

If Israel, in particular, is incapable of adapting itself to the age of individualism, what happened to the kibbutz on a micro level will happen to the country on a macro level. A reverse Darwinian process occurred on the kibbutz because it was incapable of seeing individuals as their own justification; that the aim and purpose of the kibbutz was supposed to be to optimize self-actualization. Thus, many of the best and brightest left the kibbutz. Unless Israel adapts itself to the individual's desire for self-actualization through excellence, a mass emigration of the best and brightest will occur. The loss of these individuals will jeopardize Israel no less than Arab and Moslem threats.

GLOBAL PARADOX AND ZIONIST VISIONS

Collective well-being depends on optimizing the individual well-being of increasing numbers of Jewish individuals. The concept of Zionism as centered on some absolutist concept of national sovereignty has become anachronistic and increasingly out of touch with the reality of how the Jews actually live their lives as Jewish individuals, Jewish communities, and a Jewish country. We are all, whether we like it or not, part of the new reality of global trade and labor markets held together by an integrated global telecommunications system.

We are obliged to adapt to this new global environment if we wish to prosper. This new environment has reduced the significance of the nation-state to the national collective's well-being. The paradox is that in order to strengthen the nation-state's ability to serve its citizens as well as the national collective we must surrender many aspects of sovereignty and state monopoly on power. This is because the nation-state is no longer the primary organizing feature of humanity. Regional frameworks such as the European Union and NAFTA, global economic frameworks such as the WTO, IMF, and World Bank, international political frameworks such as the United Nations, and innumerable bilateral and multilateral economic and political agreements have replaced the nation-state as the dominant organizing feature of human society. National egoism is now cultivating a desire on the part of thinking governments to become members in good standing of as many regional, international, and global organizations as possible.

One of the greatest challenges facing the Jewish people in the 21st century will be how to relate to this new global circumstance. Perhaps the traditional concept of the Jews as a global community, a concept contrary to classical Zionism, should be revisited.

REINVENTING THE DIASPORA

The most obvious implication is the need to give up the concept of "negation of the Diaspora" as one of the central Zionist tenets. The global Jewish community should be celebrating the unprecedented options now open to the Jewish people – those who want to live in Israel, those who want to live outside of Israel and those who want to have one foot in Israel and one foot in the Diaspora (which may one day be the majority of Jews).

All of these options are legitimate and should become acceptable to a reconstructed Zionist ideology in the 21st century. World Jewry and Israel should sanction this new reality. A reconstructed Zionist ideology ought to give intellectual coherence to this developing global Jewish consciousness.

Such a development requires a rethinking of the entire concept of the Israeli émigré or *yored*. We live in a highly mobile world with new "tribes" of nomadic skilled professionals moving to greener pastures of professional advancement as a way of life. These moves may be for years or even decades. Increasing numbers of skilled Israelis are becoming part of global professional tribes and are discovering that in order to actualize themselves as individuals they must spend years and decades outside of Israel.

Highly skilled individuals now "shop" for countries to live in much as they once looked for stores to shop in. But this should not be cause for Zionist despair. Israel's dynamic and interesting economy can offer Jews in these global professional tribes the opportunity to spend years and decades in Israel. Moreover, the dispersion of professional Israelis around the world should be cultivated as a cultural asset to local Jewish communities, just as Western Jews in Israel could be cultivated as a civic asset to local Israeli communities. It is time to exploit the value of the *yored*. The Israeli Diaspora could become a conduit through which Diaspora professionals connect to Israel, spending parts of their professional lives actually working or cyber-working in Israel.

FROM ALTRUISTIC TO SELF-INTEREST ZIONISM

Spending work time in Israel would not be a "donation" and would not constitute self-sacrifice in the name of a greater cause. It would be an integral part of professional and individual development, comparable to professional Israelis living and working outside of Israel. A new Zionist might call this *intellectual aliya*. The vast power of the Internet could enable professional Jews around the world to become an integral part of an Israeli/Jewish knowledge-brokering infrastructure that could import information, transform this into knowledge products, and export it to customers all over the world.

Israel could perform the same function in reverse for its global Jewish partners. None of this would be based on altruism; all of it would be based on mutual self-interest. The Quakers used to have a saying, "doing well by doing good." Non-altruistic Zionism would reverse this into *"doing good by doing well."* This does not mean a self-indulgent glorification of one's own desires at the expense of everyone else. It simply means that each individual is not only a value unto himself or herself but also, because of the rapid rate of change, the most necessary component of the new global reality. Paradoxically, as the human community becomes more unified within the emergent global system, the individual becomes more important and, because of information technology, more powerful.

This does not challenge Israel's importance or its special significance for world Jewry. Simply, the nation-state's significance is being transformed from a political, economic, and social entity to an entity dedicated to the preservation and development of a particular ethnic culture as well as to the well-being of its citizens as individuals. Israel is still of central importance, even as the very concept of geographic centrality becomes obsolete within the concept of network. All nodes are not equal. Some are more important than others, depending on situation and historical context. Israel is unique. If you doubt this, conduct the following mental experiment: Try to imagine a Jewish future if Israel were to disappear, then try to imagine a Jewish future if any other Jewish community were to disappear; more important, try to envisage a Jewish future if Israel develops into a third-rate, mediocre country.

As my friend and colleague Rabbi/Dr. Moshe Dror has noted: *Tsion*, the root of *Tsionut* (that is, Zionism), comes from *tsayen*, which means "to point out." From this, we derive the word *lehitstayen*, which means "that which is worthy of being pointed out" or to excel.

One expression of a new-Zionist vision might be to empower a generation of Jews to fulfill their passion for individual and social excellence by way of the Zionist project no matter where they might live. This has surprising implications for the very concept of Zionism. If Zionism (*Tsionut*) can be seen as a synonym for excellence, then mediocrity or satisfaction with mediocrity is in its very essence anti-Zionist. Israel, in its present mediocre state, is therefore an anti-Zionist entity. The Jewish paradox is that it has become the task of the Diaspora to assist Israel to *Zionize* itself – to achieve excellence. How can we make this enlightened vision a reality? *HaRashoot Netuna* – it is up to us.

"...few demands are as uncomfortable...disquieting or fearful as the call to innovate"

Dr. Elsie Clews Parsons

| PART II |

REALIZATION:
LOOKING BACK FROM 2020

The following chapters are an imagineered future written from the perspective of 2020. As mentioned in the Introduction, I have borrowed this device from Herzl's *Old New Land* and from Edward Bellamy's 19th century classic *Looking Backward: From 2000 to 1887*. Unlike Bellamy, the time span difference is only 13 years and not 113 years. This enables me to make more believable connections between present reality and the desired future. I believe that any vision of the future longer than several decades risks drifting into wishful thinking and fantasy.

Wishful thinking and fantasy are not in themselves negatives. They are part and parcel of the "hope springs eternal" trait inherent to the human condition, without which civilization would be greatly impoverished. In other contexts, I have allowed myself the luxury of imagining human realities centuries into the future. But such flights of imagination would not be useful for the ambitions I have for this book. It is my immodest aspiration that this book be transformative – that it give the Jews an inkling as how *through their own efforts* and by way of existing Jewish organizations and initiatives they might create a better *immediate* future for themselves and for their children. This is not a book that says: "Gee, I hope things get better because things are really bad right now". It is a book that says: "Look, this is what we can begin to do now in order to make things better".

While writing these chapters I was stunned to discover how many initiatives, projects and organizations in the Diaspora and in Israel already exist that support my fundamental argument. I have incorporated many of them into the description of my imagined future. I have done this for several reasons. First, to give credit where credit is due to initiatives that most of world Jewry is unaware of. Second and more important as concrete support for the ideas I present in this part. In polishing the final version of these chapters I have come across even more initiatives and organizations that support my vision. I have not included these because there comes a point in writing at which one must stop and finish. Existing organizations are cited with their websites. Organizations which I imagineer as part of my future vision appear without a website.

In a way this discovery was ego-deflating – I am not so original after all. Yet in another way this discovery was both exhilarating and useful. Exhilarating because it gives hope that these ideas will find greater acceptance, and useful because many building blocks for this future vision *already* exist. I have tried to connect the dots between these existing projects in order to present a coherent model of a desirable Jewish future. My aim is to focus energy, excite imagination and inspire action.

I have favored the practical over the moralistic because I agree with Benjamin Franklin that being practical is more moral than being moralistic. If something is not practical it will not be implemented, if it is not implemented it cannot be moral. Or as Franklin's biographer Richard Morris would have put it "what is moral is what works and what works is moral". I want the future of the Jews to be noble and good, secure and flourishing, meaningful and worthwhile. These aims must find concrete expression if they are to be achieved.

The following chapters are my view as to how this might be done. They are part of the story of how the Jewish people can reinvent themselves and lay the foundations for a thriving new Jewish civilization.

THE REASSERTION OF THE DIASPORA

One of the most significant developments of the past 12 years has been the reassertion of the Diaspora, led by American Jewry but reenforced by a resurgent European Jewry. This was stimulated by a growing uneasiness with the leadership and direction Israel was providing to the Jewish people at large. The second Lebanese war and concurrent governmental scandals were the immediate triggers. A major subtext was the growing resentment of many Diaspora Jews at being treated as supplementary to Israel's needs and the negative effects this was having on the identification of young Diaspora Jews with anything Jewish.

When this process began over a decade ago the advocates of post-Zionism celebrated. Yet in retrospect we can see a historical irony. This reassertion of the Diaspora has been essentially Zionist. It has been characterized by the Diaspora demanding that Israel become an instrument for the entire Jewish people and Israel ultimately agreeing to this demand. Consequently, a new partnership was born.

This meant that Israel and the Diaspora would work as equals to develop institutions and frameworks that would guarantee meaningful Jewish existence. The new partnership replaced three existing realities:

- The Diaspora as supplementary to the needs of Israel (fundraising, political lobbying etc.),

- the Diaspora as a self contained cultural entity with no need for Israel,
- but most of all a growing indifference to Jewish identity and Israel.

This indifference was the primary driving force behind the new partnership. Increased numbers of young Diaspora Jews were becoming indifferent to Israel and to Jewish life and identity in general. They no longer cared one way or the other. Many young Israelis were also becoming indifferent to solidarity with world Jewry and Jewish identity as opposed to Israeli identity. The new partnership reversed this trend. It created new frameworks for relating to Israel and expressing Jewish identity and thus rejuvenated Zionism.

IMPACT ON ISRAEL AND ZIONISM

The concept of Israel as the instrument of the entire Jewish people produced a robust new brand of Zionist thinking. *The primary aim of classical Zionism had been to create a Jewish State. The primary aim of the new Zionism was to reconstruct the Diaspora by reconstructing Israel-Diaspora relations.* Zionism became the property of the entire Jewish People and Israel was the primary beneficiary. A now famous essay entitled *"What is this Nonsense about the Negation of the Diaspora"* (2010) served as a major intellectual justification for this new concept. The author of the essay, an American born *Israeli*, made the following observations.

> There are more Jews in Israel than Irish in Ireland, Finns in Finland, Norwegians in Norway and Danes in Denmark and these countries do not have trouble sustaining a vigorous national culture based on a high standard of living. Nor are they obsessively preoccupied with the size of their population. Why do we Israelis continue to feel that bringing more Jews to Israel is such a vital national goal? Is it the internal threat of the Israeli Arab birthrate? This has been declining for almost two decades because of the rise

in the standard of living and greatly improved educational level of Israeli Arab women. A universal sociological rule is that educated women have smaller families. Educated Arab women in Israel today already have a lower birthrate than the Jews.

What we Israelis have that the Finns, Norwegians and Danes (and even the Irish) do not, is a well developed and powerful Diaspora so intimately concerned with our welfare. This is a strategic resource that is the envy of every nation on earth and we Zionists – at least ideologically – want to do away with it. *In the course of human events has there ever been an ideological principle so irrational?*

A new breed of Diaspora leaders arose in response to this new approach: leaders reminiscent of Weizmann, Brandeis, Hillel Silver and Wise. This in turn caused Israeli leaders to take a different direction. The headline in the New York Times said it all: *Israeli Prime Minister tells Jews: "Don't Send Us Money– Invest in your Local Communities"*. Another prominent Israeli public figure added: "We don't want your contributions we want your ideas and initiatives."

While many of the projects discussed below were first conceived by Israeli thinkers, Diaspora Jews initiated and implemented them. They possessed the energy, idealism and intellectual force. Israelis had been intellectually overstretched for decades. They had been carrying a self imposed load dictated by the outworn Zionist principle of "negation of the Diaspora". Zionist purists and would be ideologues called this development "a betrayal of Zionism". What it has proven to be is the opposite. It has been a maturation of Zionist ideology that has enabled the realization of the Zionist project on a scale and of a quality that Herzl, the dreamer, would have found incredible. It was named the *New Zionism*. The contribution to Jewish life has been enormous. Just as women's liberation added 50% of society's underutilized populations to the development of their societies, so too the addition of the talents and energies of the previously *underutilized*

Diaspora (50% of the Jewish people) contributed to the development of Israel and world Jewry.

The paradox was that *New Zionism* facilitated the aims of classic Zionism, most notably in the area of demographics. The improvement in Israel's standard of living and quality of life it made possible greatly lessened emigration for economic and professional reasons. It also created the conditions for increased *aliya* from the West. As of this writing (2020), a thousand European and American Jews are arriving in Israel weekly – over 50,000 a year. Contrary to the conventional wisdom of classical Zionism this development is not negating Jewish life in the Diaspora but reinforcing it. Every one of these immigrants becomes a focal point of concern for Israel for a wide range of family and friends left behind.

This concern has in many cases translated into more active participation in the local Jewish community. Recent research has shown that in 90% of the immigrants' immediate families at least one member becomes active in a Jewish organization or activity within one year of their immigration. Immigration to Israel is not a zero sum game. Addition to Israel is not subtraction from the Diaspora. Within the framework of the *New Zionism* it has become a win-win situation whereby the Diaspora is also strengthened. The fact is that immigration of friends and family to Israel has become a major barrier to assimilation for those remaining in the Diaspora. One cannot be for *aliya* and for the negation of the Diaspora as *aliya* strengthens the Diaspora.

New Zionism has played a major role in the Diaspora reversing its demographic decline. Because of new partnership projects a significantly higher number of young Jews began to seek out Jewish activities. A much higher percentage of non-Jewish spouses also chose to become members of the Jewish people. A new organization called *Ruth* was established. It was the official "welcome mat" for these new

Jews. Based on the principles of the biblical story of the Moabite woman Ruth welcomed into the People of Israel by Naomi, it offered a warm embrace to non-Jewish spouses rather than the cold shoulder often previously experienced.

The Society for Humanistic Judaism www.shj.org has become the preferred option for agnostic non-Jewish spouses to join the Jewish people by way of a "conversion" ceremony that affirms certain general principles and a commitment to dedicate oneself to *Tikkun Olam* and the welfare of the Jewish community wherever it may be. This corresponds to the idea of Jewish citizenship discussed previously. The increased community identification of non-Jewish spouses has also become a major component in the reversal of demographic erosion.

Intermarriage has now become a major positive factor for Jewish demographics. The Jewish spouse more times than not remains Jewish and the non-Jewish spouse, more times than not, identifies with the community. For the first time since before WWII the Diaspora is now experiencing a net demographic gain despite substantial *aliya* to Israel. This has reversed the Jewish reality of two decades earlier, when the western Diaspora was experiencing net demographic decline despite substantial immigration from Russia and Israel.

Israel now has a population of 8 million Jews and 2 million Arab citizens (20% of the population). As a consequence of educational affirmative action for Arab women enacted in 2009 the birthrates of both communities are now similar. Given continued Jewish immigration and equal birthrates, the percentage of Arab citizens will decline to 15% by 2030. The economic, professional, cultural and social profile of Israel's Arab citizens is now on a par with that of Jewish citizens.

This equalization of circumstances joined to the end of the "demographic threat" has enabled both communities to interrelate as equals and has all but ended structural and cultural racism in Israel. Israeli Arabs have become a *"light unto Ishmael"* – a model for other Arab societies throughout the Middle East. This too has been an indirect consequence of the reassertion of the Diaspora.

THE ISRAELI DIASPORA

The major player in this new partnership has been the half million strong *Israeli Diaspora*, the most vilified group in the classical Zionist narrative. From being "traitors" to Israel and Zionism they became the bonding agent that held the new partnership together. They have facilitated constructive communication, being able to speak the psychological language of each. In truth they were the major initiators of this new approach. They had been a growing subset within Jewish organizations and embraced the new partnership when it was conceived. They made their participation in Jewish organizations conditional on engaging in special projects that reflected the new partnership concept. They were the pioneers of this new Jewish reality.

The *Israeli Diaspora* initiated the projects and soon a growing number of native born American Jews began to join them. A prime example of this phenomenon was the *Jewish Energy Project* described in the following chapter. This was initiated by a group of Israeli high tech executives in Silicon Valley that had been enlisted by the *Set America Free Coalition* www.setamericafree.org to pressure the government to adapt the coalition's agenda. (One of the founders of the coalition was himself an Israeli American). It seems that being on the margins of society gives one a greater perspective. Being in a society one can not see the forest through the trees. This truism enabled the Jews to see new opportunities in American society and Israeli Americans to see new opportunities in Jewish society.

Major players in this development were *The Israeli-American Study Initiative* www.israelisinamerica.org; and *The Council of Israeli Community* www.cicisrael.org. Much of the online debate and philosophical discussion about this new development took place on www.newzionist.com founded by Israeli Americans and on *Zeek: A Jewish Journal of Thought and Culture* www.zeek.net. In aggregate, Israeli Diaspora individuals and organizations were the driving force in creating this new reality.

RELIGIOUS PLURALISM

A new reality regarding the question of religious pluralism in Israel developed. At the outset of the second decade of the 21st century, the Conservative and Reform Movements became militant. This combination of Reform and Conservative militancy along with the rise of *Humanistic Judaism* caused a shift in the religious landscape of Israel. These three movements as well as the Reconstructionists have been recognized in Israel as legitimate constituents of the Jewish people with rights equal to the Orthodox. This was enabled by a reaffirmation of the Enlightenment principle of separation of "synagogue" and state. As one Israeli thinker paraphrased Lincoln: "the Jewish people cannot exist half for religious freedom and half in contravention of religious freedom". He added that separation of synagogue and state is not the same as separation of religion from state. Judaism is still the official religion of the Jewish state (in the same way that Lutheranism is the official religion of the Swedish State) but, *unlike* Sweden, the clerical class has no special status and is not directly employed or subsidized by the State.

Religious affairs budgets are now distributed to every citizen of Israel on a proportional basis by way of electronic cards for purposes of contributions to religious institutions only, according to the religious preferences of the individual citizen. There is no longer any direct State involvement in religious institutions or governance. The Chief Rabbinate (an artifice created by the British Empire and elected by the Knesset) has faded into history. Citizens now use their cards to make yearly contributions to the religious body of their choice. Money not used is returned to the State. All non-Orthodox movements can now legally conduct marriages in Israel, which by law must be registered by the Ministry of Interior. And since many agnostic Israelis have been joining *The Society for Humanistic Judaism* the conflict between Jewish and Israeli identity, which had been worrying Israeli society since its inception has diminished. If the Diaspora had not reasserted itself, religious equality in Israel would have remained a dead letter and the divide between "being Jewish" and "being Israeli" would have widened.

EUROPEAN JEWRY

European Jewry, led by British Jewry, has also played a vital role in the reassertion of the Diaspora as an equal participant in the cause of Jewish well-being. In 2008, British Jews were central to the establishment of *The Society for a Sane and Democratic Asia (SSDA)*. It was initially composed of Jews, Hindus and Sikhs – British minorities whose persons and property had been declared legitimate targets of violence by radical British Muslims. These groups especially were psychologically united in a feeling of growing isolation within British society due to the disproportionate attention (some called it pandering) being paid to the Moslem community. If they didn't feel physically beset they felt psychologically beset. Very quickly the small Chinese community joined them – especially Buddhists who hadn't forgotten or forgiven the cultural atrocity perpetuated on the statues of Buddha in Afghanistan by advocates of the same Islamic Fascism that was raising its head in Great Britain.

Before long, many moderate Moslems who were disgusted with the way Islamic Fascism had disgraced their culture joined the Society as well. The analogy was made to Willy Brandt, Thomas Mann, Marlene Dietrich and others who saved German honor during the dark days of Nazism.

Quickly the *SSDA* equaled the Muslim community in size and became a comparable voice in British public discourse. British Jewry wisely adopted a strategy of indirect approach and took a role secondary to the other ethnic participants in public debate. A Sikh or Hindu (or modern Moslem) protesting against England becoming Londonstan always had more impact. These groups were also impervious to charges of racism by the postmodern left (unlike Zionist Jews).

The Jewish communities of continental Europe formed similar alliances with non-Moslem and moderate Moslem minority groups. Many of these activities have been coordinated by the *European Jewish Congress* www.eurojewcong.org based on research and policy papers prepared by the *Institute for Jewish Policy Research* www.jpr. org.uk. This concerted action quickly led to a strategic decision to focus on energy as the key threat to the Jewish People. A European Branch of the *Jewish Energy Project* was established (see next chapter). They became a central force in the establishment of the *Set Europe Free Coalition* which was created as an affiliate of the *Set America Free Coalition*. Their aim was to wean Europe from OPEC oil.

NORTH AMERICAN JEWRY

North American Jewry took the lead in redefining the Diaspora. In 2008 the *American Jewish World Service* www.ajws.org joined forces with the *Jewish Coalition for Service* www.jewishservice.org and other Jewish organizations identified with www.socialaction.com to form the *Jewish Service Federation*. The *Federation* transformed NGO philosophy and operating procedures by developing practical applications for the multi-purpose project approach to problem solving. Their projects have since been imitated by NGOs around the world.

Three main projects reflected the social imagination and energy of American Jewry at this time: *Urban Plantations, Tikkun Olam Boarding Schools Project* for AIDS orphans and street children in the Third World as well as the *Get them off the Grid Project*.

URBAN PLANTATIONS

This is a for profit company, wholly owned by the *Jewish Service Federation*. The company makes use of empty lots and flat roofs of buildings in the inner cities of the United States to grow a wide variety of vegetables using Israeli drip irrigation and hot house technology. It employs mostly Black and Hispanic teenagers and is coordinated with local clergy and community activists. It has become a major economic activity in many communities. And while it is not organic farming in its purist sense it has won kudos from environmentalists because it uses one tenth the pesticides, chemical fertilizers and water required by conventionally grown field crops. These savings are one of the advantages of Israeli drip irrigation systems. The professional aspects of the program are supervised by Israel's *Volcani Institute of Agricultural Research* http://www.agri.gov.il as well as representatives from the Religious Kibbutz Movement www.kdat.org.il. Religious kibbutzniks are preferred because market research indicated that a natural 'export' market for the produce (in addition to the 'domestic' market of the communities themselves) was the kosher food market. The relatively closed system of growing enables the marketing of produce free of non-kosher pests.

The company complies with immigration and minimum wage laws and requested the *United Farm Workers* www.ufw.org to organize their workers. The company and the union cooperate in conducting enrichment courses designed to increase the skill level (and salaries) of the workers. They commissioned ORT www.ort.org to design and run the enrichment courses. Since ORT was founded on the philosophy that handouts don't work but that teaching a skill is a step to improving one's chance for success in life, this was a natural project for them.

The combination of disciplined work, on the job training and opportunity for advancement as well as citizenship skills developed in union activity has had a profound quantitative and qualitative impact on many inner city communities. *Urban Plantations* is now a significant customer for Israel's agricultural technology exports, creating several thousand well paying jobs in Israel. The company has insisted that its Israeli suppliers give hiring priority to Arab, particularly Bedouin women. Over a thousand minority women in Israel have achieved economic independence as a result. This coincided nicely with Israel's new social development policy which had identified the low status of women in minority and religious sectors as being key to addressing economic, social and cultural dilemmas in Israeli society.

The company also makes enough profit so that its constituent organizations do not have to spend time fundraising. They are free to expand their activities in other directions and develop other projects.

THE TIKKUN OLAM BOARDING SCHOOL PROJECT

One of these projects is the *Tikkun Olam Boarding School Project* for street children and AIDS orphans around the world. The *Jewish Services Federation* in cooperation with the *Israel Forum for International Humanitarian Aid* (IsraAID) http://www.israaid.org.il and *World Jewish Aid* in the United Kingdom http://www.worldjewishaid.org set up three exemplar projects; one in Africa, one in Latin America and one in Eastern Europe. The boarding schools were uniform turnkey installations each accommodating 1,000 children.

The *Jewish Service Federation* then devoted all its energies to enlisting Jewish managerial talent to expand the project at a rapid pace. The aim was to "franchise" the concept and have additional boarding schools sponsored by other NGOs and private companies doing business in these geographical areas. The thinking was that if MacDonald's and Starbucks could open a branch a day, *The Tikkun Olam Boarding School System* could also open a school a day. At present a *Tikkun Olam Boarding School* is being opened every day around the world and more than three million children are being accommodated.

Jewish fast food industry executives also established a training college for staff to manage and teach in the boarding schools. Their organizational models were the training "colleges" of the fast food industry, such as McDonald's "Hamburger University". (McDonald's itself has sponsored several hundred Boarding Schools and has stimulated competition amongst the rest of the fast food industry which has sponsored over a thousand schools.) Course content, professional supervision and quality control is under the auspices of ORT. The *Tikkun Olam Training College* in the United States has recently been accredited by the *Middle States Association of Colleges and Schools* as a two year managerial and pedagogical Junior College.

The Israeli branch is part of the ORT chain of colleges in Israel and has been accredited as a full fledged Teachers Seminar permitted to issue a B.Ed. by the Israeli Ministry of Education. Many graduates of the American Junior College are now completing their B.A. degree at the Israeli branch by a combination of distance learning and short, intensive residence programs in the summer.

These original pilot projects were self-sufficient in energy, vegetables, poultry and eggs using Israeli technology. Many of the subsequent boarding schools, being turnkey franchise units, followed suit and once again a very large market was established for these Israeli technologies and once again thousands of well paying jobs were created for minority women in Israel.

All the boarding schools are profit centers because they provide the human resources of sugarcane plantations and sugar beet farms that produce ethanol or butanol as partial substitutes for gasoline. They have become a central component of the Energy Project described in the next chapter. And this is what has driven their rapid expansion. Major chains like Wal-Mart, MacDonald's and others have established ethanol and butanol service stations in their parking lots. Their "contributions" to the boarding schools they sponsor are really business investments guaranteeing a growing supply of product to a profitable branch of their business activity. It is this profitability that has made the project systemic and self-sustaining and not contingent on intermittent and untrustworthy altruistic instincts of a fickle and easily bored public.

The production of butanol is a case of historical irony. Its production process uses the bacterium *Clostridium acetobutylicum*, which is also known as the *Weizmann organism*. It was Chaim Weizmann who first used this bacterium for the production of acetone from starch in 1916. The main use of acetone was the making of Cordite which was the main component of explosives at the time. Britain had been dependent on German chemical industry for acetone (not a convenient situation when you are at war with them). Weizmann liberated the British from this dependence. Many historians believe that Weizmann's contribution to the British war effort in WWI was a major reason why he was able to obtain the Balfour Declaration. Butanol was a by-product of this same process. Thus from the grave Chaim Weizmann has made another major contribution to Jewish well being.

GET THEM OFF THE GRID PROJECT

The *Get them off the Grid Project* was a late development of the Jewish Energy Project described in detail in the following chapter. *The United Jewish Communities* www.ujc.org, was convinced *by Israel* to divert funds previously set aside for Israel to Native American communities. The funds were used to buy Israeli alternative energy technologies with the express purpose of removing Native American communities from the energy grids making them self-sufficient in energy. The Israeli economy actually benefited from this so called "diversion" of funds. This was because economic research over the past 30 years had proven that a dollar generated in the private sector has one and half to two times more impact than public spending in terms of economic activity and jobs created.

THE $1,000 CLUB

The centrality of fundraising in Israel-Diaspora relations had not only distorted the relationship but had also impeded the vitality of the Diaspora communities. It had signaled to those not independently wealthy that they were less important. Leadership had been equated with the size of one's contribution.

In 2007 a private firm, *Ziv Group Ltd.* www.zivgroup.co.il, a small Israeli translation company, came up with a different concept. They initially listed themselves on a special website set up by the Israel Export Institute to export non-tangible services http://professional-services-israel.export.gov.il/. This proved to be a non-starter until they expanded on the concept by finding Diaspora representatives to sell their services for a 10% commission.

They promoted this with a variation of the old Quaker saying "doing well by doing good". Their version was "doing good by doing well". Their message was that if you have earned a thousand dollars by selling Israeli services you have pumped $10,000 into Israel's economy. They further claimed (a claim supported by economists) that this would be the equivalent of $15,000 of economic activity generated by donations (for the same reasons cited above).

Almost immediately dozens of competitors and other companies dealing in a variety of non tangible services (graphics, animation etc.) followed the *Ziv Group* example. If a Diaspora Jew made $10,000 by this method it means he or she had "contributed" $100,000 ($150,000 equivalence) to Israel's economy. In this way, teachers, legal secretaries, cab drivers etc. became movers and shakers within the local Jewish community and improved their own financial situation along the way. Today over one billion dollars of Israel service exports are generated annually by this method and tens of thousands of Diaspora Jews are adding to their income and strengthening their Jewish identity by promoting the Israeli economy. The Israeli Diaspora was especially active in this initiative, in particular *The Israeli Business Network* www.ibnbh.org. Wealthier people are contributing their Israeli profits to local causes. In this way the $1,000 club is enabling Israel to contribute to Diaspora welfare in the same way that the Diaspora had been contributing to Israel.

Summing Up

Rather than resting on their laurels these rejuvenated Diaspora communities are now proactively seeking out and designing new multi-purpose projects in cooperation with each other and with Israel. The entire concept of the Israeli center and the Diaspora periphery has been revised. Jewish life is now seen as a web of activities with dozens of Jewish communities interacting with one another and with Israel. Israel and North American Jewry are still major hubs of activity and their relationship with one another is still crucial but they do not overshadow the activity of other communities. Many interesting initiatives are coming out of much smaller Jewish communities and the decade 2020-2030 promises to be even more remarkable than the decade 2010-2020.

CHAPTER 12

JEWISH ENERGY PROJECT

The first and most important venture of the new partnership was the *Jewish Energy Project*. Energy was determined to be a Jewish problem. The goal of the project was to destroy the power of petroleum as an international commodity. This has for all intents and purposes been accomplished.

Destroying the power of petroleum as an international commodity has benefited everyone, but especially the Jewish people. It seriously undermined the financing of international Islamic terror, reducing it to a minor tactical annoyance rather than the major strategic threat it had become. It also rendered impotent the petroleum funded nuclear weapons programs of rogue states such as Iran. These were the two biggest external threats to the existence of the Jewish People. Nuclear weapons were a direct threat. Terror was an indirect threat as it caused policy analysts to conclude that the very existence of Israel supported by the Jewish lobby was the problem. This view was one of the components of the new anti-Semitism, poorly disguised as anti-Zionism, which had raised its head in Europe and was spreading to certain segments of American academia.

The end of oil dependence has also been beneficial for the world economy. The U.S. trade deficit has been reduced by 40%, and hundreds of thousands of well paying domestic jobs have been created. This was in line with the 2003 *National Defense Council Foundation* report, which examined the price of imported oil in terms of the security costs associated with safeguarding supply. The report showed that the actual cost of oil was much higher than the price consumers saw at the pump and included such expenses as:

- Almost $49.1 billion in annual defense outlays to maintain the ability to defend the flow of Persian Gulf oil – the equivalent of adding $1.17 to the price of a gallon of gasoline. This did not include the cost of the second Iraq war. In other words, policing the Persian Gulf had cost U.S. taxpayers half a trillion dollars between the two Iraq wars.
- The loss of 828,400 jobs in the U.S. economy
- The loss of $159.9 billion in GNP annually.
- The loss of $13.4 billion in federal and state revenues annually.
- Total annual economic penalties of $297.2 - $304.9 billion.
- Periodic oil shocks over the course of the three decades from 1973 had cost the American economy $2 - 2.5 trillion (unpredictability is expensive).
- The twin towers atrocity. Osama Bin Laden had publicly indicated that the World Trade Center attacks were a response to the U.S. "occupation" of Saudi Arabia. The American military presence in Saudi Arabia existed to defend the house of Saud, an undemocratic regime that guaranteed the United States access to Saudi Arabian oil. The September 11 attacks resulted in more than $200 billion dollars in direct and indirect economic losses.

In 2006, the price of a barrel of oil was *triple* that of 2003. If all these hidden costs had been included in the *real* cost of oil (and not indirectly subsidized by the American taxpayer), a gallon of gasoline refined from Persian Gulf oil would have cost over $10.00. When these facts were laid before the American people and driven home in an unrelenting daily PR campaign by grassroots lobbyists, the ground swell of public opinion against oil dependence became implacable. Jewish activism in this campaign was not primary and we Jews should not even pretend to take credit for the results. A vigorous and growing coalition of social forces was already in existence. But when the full force of the Jewish lobby joined the general social alliance for energy independence it was a vital "tipping point" in the battle to free the West from hostile and unstable energy sources.

The industrial might of the United States was mobilized in a manner not seen since World War II. By 2010, a new coal-liquefaction plant (a coal-fired power plant that uses a carbon-neutral process to convert coal into a liquid fuel) producing 30,000 barrels of fuel a day (at $40 a barrel) was being installed every month in the United States. This was adding 360,000 barrels of *daily* production every year. Thermal and catalytic depolymerization units that produced the equivalent of a thousand barrels of fuel from sewage and garbage were being installed daily. This was adding 365,000 barrels of *daily* production a year. Plug in hybrids, flex fuel engines (engines capable of using ethanol or methanol mixed with conventional gasoline), household energy conservation and increased use of wind, solar and geothermal energy were *conserving* an additional 300,000 barrels of *daily* consumption of oil every year. Ethanol production from agricultural waste and bio-diesel from the food processing industry was adding the equivalent of 100,000 barrels of *daily* production of fuel a year. By 2010 more than 1,100,000 barrels of *daily* production of oil was being taken off the international market each year by the lower 48 States alone.

Given its greater dependence on imported oil, the European Union has benefited even more from this new energy reality. But the developing world, especially Africa, has benefited the most. Oil price fluctuations – caused by the OPEC oil boycotts of the 1970's and subsequent instability in the Middle East in the 90's and early 21st century – had a devastating effect on the African economy and played a major role in turning Africa into an economic basket case.

Once energy had been identified as the keystone of international development strategy, North America, the European Union and Japan began devoting 50% of their foreign aid to making "third world" countries energy independent and thus immune to the world energy price fluctuations. As a consequence sub-Saharan African, Southeast Asian and Latin American countries have all become energy independent. Moreover some of these countries have become major energy players themselves by developing huge exports in ethanol and butanol. Equatorial countries have a tremendous advantage in growing sugar cane which produces 8 units of energy for every one unit invested as opposed to corn – the major feedstock for ethanol in the United States – which produces 1.3 units of energy for every unit invested.

In the United States the African American and Hispanic communities supported by the Jewish and environmental lobbies joined forces to pressure for an end of all import taxes on ethanol and butanol. As late as 2007 the American import tax on ethanol from relatively friendly countries was 54 cents a gallon while the tax on imported oil from hostile countries was zero. This new ethanol/butanol policy was multi-dimensional. It helped liberate the United States and much of Europe from OPEC intimidation and radically decreased the funds available for terror and anti-western propaganda. It also generated a huge export industry in the poorest countries in the world (and has been a major factor in the African economic renaissance) and it was better for the environment. Today over 50% of the vehicles in the United States, the European Union and Japan have flex fuel engines that run on E85 (a mixture of 85% ethanol and 15% gasoline). By 2030 this will grow to 90%. In the newly industrialized countries of China and India it is already 90%. And since India can grow sugar cane and make gasoline from liquefied coal as well as exploit its huge potential for solar power it has also achieved energy independence.

The removal of the American import tax on ethanol took effect in 2009 after the 2008 Presidential elections. American agri-business – with tremendous interests in corn based ethanol – mounted a massive campaign against the elimination of the tax. But politicians know how to count and when the lobby for elimination of the tax represented almost 100 million Americans (Hispanics, Blacks, Jews and environmentalists) both Presidential candidates, and all congressional and Senate candidates outdid themselves in promising to do away with the tax. It was eliminated in the first 100 days of the new presidential term of office.

The United States became *completely* energy independent this past year (2020) through a combination of conservation, alternative energy (solar, wind and geothermal), gasification and liquefaction of coal, and various technologies that turn carbon-based waste (sewage, manure, garbage, plastic, rubber, agricultural, etc.) into usable diesel and gas. The United States had already become relatively energy independent by 2015 – its sole oil imports being from fellow NAFTA members Canada and Mexico. As early as 2009, the projected end of US energy dependence had enabled greater geo-political flexibility as well as greater adherence to democratic values. The era of pretending to be friends with thugs or of being intimidated by them because they sat on vast reserves of oil was finally over.

China, with its vast coal deposits, immense amount of rice and wheat straw (as ethanol feed stocks) and human waste also employed similar technologies and policies to achieve energy independence. With the United States and China becoming energy independent, large supplies of oil have been diverted to Japan, Korea and Taiwan (which had also drastically reduced oil consumption by conservation and use of bio-diesel technologies). These countries presently receive all their remaining energy imports from Russia, Canada and Mexico and not OPEC. The European Union's remaining oil and gas imports also come from non-OPEC countries such as Russia, Mexico and Brazil as well as West Africa.

The residual resentment against OPEC for its past boycotts and cartel behavior encouraged the EU and Japan to procure oil from other suppliers when it became possible. OPEC had been banking on emerging markets such as China and India but, as noted, these countries are no longer in need of OPEC oil. This has so weakened the resented organization that Nigeria and post-Chavez Venezuela left it in order to guarantee their markets. OPEC has become another weak Moslem organization similar to the Arab Boycott in effectiveness. From pumping 35% of the world's daily oil supply in 2006 it now pumps less than 10%. From threatening markets it now begs for markets.

PRACTICAL CONSEQUENCES

These developments enabled the West to stop ignoring the central role that Saudi Arabia had been playing in terror. In 2009, after the formation of OPCC (Organization of Petroleum Consuming Countries) a subtle reverse oil boycott was put into operation. The West began to slowly lessen its oil purchases from Saudi Arabia, quickly dethroning it as the biggest oil exporter in the world. By 2012 it was no longer the chief indirect financier of international Islamic terror and direct financier of anti-Western and anti-Semitic propaganda. Today exports from the Gulf (Saudi Arabia, Iran, Iraq, and Kuwait) are less than 6 million barrels a day and declining.

Ironically, the drastic downgrading of oil as an international commodity cleared the way for healthy economic, political and social developments in most of the Middle East as well as elsewhere.

Petroleum producing countries were no longer capable of ignoring global developments and international standards of governance and behavior.

In 2008, the US, EU and Japan – relying on 4 billion barrels of oil in the strategic oil reserve of the *International Energy Agency* (IEA) www.iea.org – instituted a reverse oil boycott on Iran. Within a year, Iran's oil exports were cut by half and by the beginning of 2009 were less than a million barrels a day (down from two and a half million barrels). The IEA was capable of releasing over two million barrels a day for over three years. This action quickly deprived Iran of the means to continue its nuclear development program. It also helped tame North Korea, which had been greatly dependent on Iranian purchases of their missile and weapons technology for the little foreign currency they had. Iranian financing of *Hezbollah* (never popular amongst the mass of young educated Iranians) also dried up. This had a great stabilizing effect on the Israeli-Arab conflict and was a key factor in the comprehensive peace agreement between Israel and Syria/Lebanon in 2008. This in turn defanged *Hamas* and generated a more pragmatic attitude amongst the Palestinian population which, along with other developments, generated a *modus vivendi* that continues to this day.

In 2009, its economy in collapse and its impoverished population furious, Iran underwent a second revolution. The army, intellectuals and business community became infatuated with the Turkish model of modernization and governance. The catchphrase of this second revolution was "where is the Iranian Ataturk"? Iran has since become a constitutional republic. The mullahs were relegated to their pulpits and deprived of secular power. Iran established close ties with the United States and Europe and adopted an international policy aimed at integrating into the global economy and contributing to global political stability. In 2010 it cut off all ties with terrorist organizations and in 2013 it reestablished relations with Israel.

The War on Terror and international Jihadism was not won by the direct strategy of armed intervention, but rather by the indirect strategy of destroying oil as the major international commodity. Today it is a commodity on a par with coffee, sugar and tea in terms of its impact on geopolitics.

Somewhat paradoxically, the standard of living of most of the people in the former oil powers is now higher than it was at the peak of OPEC's power. Juan Enriquez, the author of *As the Future Catches You* (Crown Publishing Group, 2000) would have predicted this outcome without difficulty. In his book he shows that countries that depend on commodities are guaranteed a future of poverty, for several reasons:

- Increased productivity and professional management had reduced the real value of commodities and natural resources in 2000 to one fifth of what they had been 150 years previously. Petroleum was a minor exception. However, the $80 a barrel oil of 2006 was still not equivalent, in real terms, to the $48 a barrel oil of 1979.

- When you have natural resources, you invest in them. When you lack them you invest in your human resources. When 70% of gross world product is the knowledge economy, investment in human resources gives a much greater return.

- Countries rich in natural resources are more likely to be ruled by corrupt and incompetent thugs or religious fanatics. Dependence on human creativity and ability requires freedom and constitutional protections. In the global knowledge economy, democracy is no longer just an ideal, it is an economic necessity. The economic situation of Saudi Arabia had already proved Enriquez's thesis. Its per capita income was $18,000 in 1982 and $9,000 in 2006.

Deprived of the economic power of their natural resource, former oil producing powers have had to reform in order to be accepted into the new global order or sink into poverty. This denied political bullies the ability to disturb the global order. Russia also had to reverse the authoritarian trends of Putin, made possible by the post 9/11 windfall oil income. Chavez of Venezuela was marginalized and lost power as the Venezuelan middle and professional classes – the only real source of development – reasserted themselves. This finally ended Peronian populism in Latin America. All Gulf oil powers have had an attack of reform, except Saudi Arabia – still dominated by *Wahabi* fanaticism – which, while turning its back on the world, no longer has the power to affect it negatively.

THE BEGINNING

As with many great historical undertakings the beginning was modest... a handful of young idealistic Jews at a parlor meeting on the East coast of the United States. They were conscious of the significance of the meeting and that they could affect the course of world history. One of those present, well read in Jewish history, noted that the first Zionist political parties in the Land of Israel – which eventually established Israel – consisted of only several dozen people.

The meeting had two distinct factions. The first was composed of 4 Jewish activists from an organization called the *Set America Free Coalition* www.setamericafree.org. This was a coalition of neo-conservatives, liberal democrats, environmental activists, evangelical Christians, involved Jews and former members of the American security and intelligence communities. Their message was concise: America's dependence on foreign oil was financing anti-American terror organizations around the world. Their solution was simple; set America free from foreign oil and we will deprive the terrorists of the financial means to conduct operations and sustain a terrorist educational system. They had put together a doable program of how this might be achieved within a decade.

They identified transportation as the chief culprit. Coal, nuclear, natural gas and alternative energy (solar, wind, geothermal etc.) would satisfy America's electricity and industrial needs. Indeed, an upgraded electricity grid would also make a big contribution to solving the transportation problem.

They were advocates of the plug-in hybrid car which at the time could travel up to 100 miles on a gallon of fuel. When manufactured with ultra light, super strong composite materials (which had become economically viable by 2014) they could travel up to 200 miles on a gallon of fuel. The fuels of choice would be varieties of diesel and gas produced from organic waste and coal or E85. They advocated that the government follow the Brazilian example and mandate that only flex fuel engines would be imported or manufactured in the United States (such a law was passed in 2009). They further estimated that a pumping apparatus for alternative fuels such as E85 could be installed in existing gas stations for as little as $60,000 per station, or less than 10 billion dollars for every gas station in the United States. The beauty of the concept was that it depended on "in place infrastructure" and did not require drastic changes in the preferences of the American motorist. It was logical, technologically feasible and doable in a short period of time.

The second faction was composed of a dozen members of a new Jewish organization called *Kol Dor* www.koldor.org. This Hebrew term has a double connotation in English: *"Voice of a Generation"* and *"The Entire Generation"*. The entire generation referred to all young Jews (under 40) in Israel and the Diaspora, intimating that young Israelis and Diaspora Jews were going to be active together as equals and that this organization was going to be the voice of this concept.

Kol Dor had been looking for a major project to exploit the energies and excite the inherent idealism of an entire generation of Jews. They realized that unless they found such a project, they would remain a small discussion group. Their ambition, however, was to become a major factor in Jewish life. The idea of the *Jewish Energy Project* inspired them to meet with the Jewish representatives of the *Set America Free Coalition*. At that meeting the *Jewish Energy Project* was born.

STRATEGY

They operated on several avenues of activity simultaneously. They conducted information campaigns and encouraged other Jewish organizations (AIPAC, Hadassah, Federation Movements etc.) to endorse the *Set America Free* agenda and to make this Jewish endorsement known to local, state and national politicians. They encouraged individual Jews to become dues paying members of *Set America Free* and to lobby for endorsements and individual memberships from non-Jewish organizations of which they were members or had good working relations with (Rotary, Lions, American Legion, Veterans of Foreign Wars, Evangelical Christians, etc.). Their aim was to make *Set America Free* the largest membership organization and strongest lobby in the United States. Their strategy succeeded. The addition of the Jewish lobby to the *Set America Free* agenda and the way this was leveraged in the non-Jewish community has been seen as a turning point in the battle against oil dependence.

They also organized a letter writing campaign to congressmen and senators, state representatives and local officials pressuring them to implement relevant aspects of the *Set America Free* program. For example:

1. Insisting that all governmental (national, state and local) non-

emergency vehicles should be plug-in hybrids with flex fuel engines. As this is a huge market, the introduction of this policy motivated the world's major car makers to produce these vehicles. The subsequent large production volume lowered the price of each unit, making it attractive to the private consumer, who realized that the fuel savings actually made these vehicles cheaper than standard engine vehicles,

2. Insisting on tax breaks for these vehicles at national, state and local levels: income tax write offs for purchase, lower state automobile registration fees and lower local parking fees,

3. Insisting on a policy to make government buildings (national, state, local) as energy self-sufficient as possible. This policy created a huge market for solar, wind and geothermal energy as well as insulation, alternative lighting technologies and smart materials such as windows that heat in the winter and cool in the summer. This huge aggregate market generated large production volume which lowered per unit costs, making it affordable for the private consumer. The home improvements industry (Home Depot, Lowes etc. and their suppliers) was an important allied lobby in pushing this legislation through,

4. Insisting on local property tax discounts for private homes that become energy self-sufficient and gas stations that install flex-fuel pumps. Lobbying the Federal Government to help underwrite this policy.

5. Insisting that local municipalities install thermal or catalytic depolymerization units turning all local sewage and garbage into useable diesel and gas. The savings on sewage treatment and garbage collection as well as the tax producing use of former landfills along with the sale of fuel produced made this economically feasible.

IMPLEMENTATION

Concurrently, European members of *Kol Dor* initiated the establishment of a *Set Europe Free Coalition*. Europe is close to achieving energy independence. It has greatly increased deployment of E85 flex fuel engines and made significant progress in the development of smart materials. Lighting and appliances technologies have become much more energy efficient. There have also been significant developments in environmentally safe exploitation of methane hydrates. Europe hopes to achieve full energy independence from hostile, dictatorial and unstable regimes in the near future. Japan is also close to achieving this aim.

The 2008 American elections as well as various European elections during this period were framed by these concerns. Politicians competed with one another and political contributions were made on the basis of candidates' positions on this issue. The new American President's inaugural speech was reminiscent of President Kennedy's man on the moon speech: "By the end of the coming decade the United States will be energy self-sufficient". He referenced *The Apollo Alliance* www.apolloalliance.org (modeled on the Man on the Moon project). The country, sick of being blackmailed by thugs, of having to live with terrorists and of being periodically obliged to spill blood because of the geographic location of oil, mobilized behind this national goal.

In Europe, the new Prime Minister of Great Britain and President of France joined with the German Chancellor to declare European Energy Independence to be Europe's equivalent of the American Man on the Moon project.

In 2009 the EU, America and Japan formed OPCC (Organization of Petroleum Consuming Countries). This was a consumer cartel formed to prevent OPEC from drastically cutting oil prices at crucial times in order to bankrupt alternative energy projects. Saudi Arabia had been frank about the use of this strategy. Some members of the government had bragged: "We will wait until you invest huge amounts of money and effort and then drastically reduce the price of oil. Not only will you lose a great deal of money but you will be inhibited for decades from trying to become energy independent".

Some research claimed that the plummeting of the price of oil to $10 dollars a barrel during the later years of the Clinton administration was a calculated ploy intended to drive low production high cost domestic wells out of the market. Since about 30,000 wells capable of producing about a half a million barrels a day (what ANWR would have produced at its peak) were capped as a consequence, one cannot dismiss the claim out of hand.

To forestall this tactic, OPCC agreed on a $70 dollar a barrel benchmark price for all oil consumed in member countries whether imported or domestically produced. The instrument for guaranteeing this price was a sliding excise tax on oil. If oil was being dumped by Saudi Arabia at $30 a barrel, an excise tax of $40 would be added at the port of entry. Domestic producers would have a similar add-on at the well head. This stabilized the petroleum market and enabled entrepreneurs and corporations to make long term energy investments without fear of having their investments sabotaged at a crucial time. Most of all, it guaranteed the viability of investments in alternative energy over the long haul.

THE ISRAEL ENERGY PROJECT

While all this was going on, the *Israel Energy Project* was initiated. Israeli members of *Kol Dor* convinced the *Young Leadership of the United Jewish Communities* that since the aggregate impact of the Diaspora's financial contribution to Israel was now only marginal; the only way to make a truly significant contribution was to design a project that would excite the imagination of young Jews while addressing a myriad of issues. The *Young Leadership*, anxious to make their own mark on Jewish life, was convinced and thus the *Israel Energy Project* was born.

The project was structured in the following way. Diaspora contributions were transferred to an Israeli non-profit organization that bought Israeli manufactured alternative energy equipment (such as produced by *Ormat* www.ormat.com and *Solel Solar Systems* www.solel.com). This injected hundreds of millions of dollars per year into these industries and created thousands of skilled well paying jobs which absorbed many workers who had previously been working in low paying manufacturing jobs.

The equipment was then donated to homes and farms of the poorest segments of the Israeli population – Jews and Arabs, without discrimination. This eliminated their energy expenses (electricity, heating, cooling and cooking) and in many cases provided additional income, as surplus energy could be sold back to the grid. The creation of thousands of well paying jobs as well as energy self-sufficient and surplus energy producing homes lifted tens of thousands over the poverty line and had a significant impact on reducing Israeli poverty.

These industries quickly developed into export industries. Their products became a major supplier of *Set America Free* and *Set Europe Free*. In America, many synagogues and sympathetic churches decided to become energy self-sufficient using solar and geo-thermal or other suitable Israeli technology. A donor would contribute a unit of the most suitable Israeli technology and get a multi-dimensional benefit: a substantial tax deduction for the cost of the contribution, a significant reduction of the energy expenses of his house of worship, a contribution to Israel's economy and reduction of Israeli poverty, as well as a contribution to making production costs of these technologies economically feasible for the general market.

This, along with other independent energy developments, has also enabled Israel to approach energy independence. These developments include an Israeli innovation that enables the extraction of oil from Israel's large shale deposits for less than 20$ a barrel as well as the splicing of mangrove tree genes onto sugar cane enabling large scale planting of sugar cane that can be irrigated by saline water. Israel's entire fleet is now flex fuel running on E85 (the gasoline component refined from the shale oil). Israeli sugar cane has now become a major agricultural export to arid countries.

As a consequence of all this, Israel has benefited environmentally, economically and socially. These alternative energy investments created many high paying jobs, enabling Israel to dispense with undercapitalized, poorly managed industrial sectors dependent on minimum wage labor. Israel's PR and standing in world opinion has increased tremendously as a consequence of this project.

With its original goals now achieved, the founding team of the *Jewish Energy Project/Kol Dor* is looking for the next project to engage their generation for the benefit of the Jewish People and the world at large.

| CHAPTER 13 |

UPGRADING ISRAEL

Neither Israeli nor Diaspora supporters of the new partnership denied the central place Israel played in Jewish life. There was general agreement that it was imperative to upgrade every aspect of Israeli society in order to enable it to perform its proper function in the service of the Jewish People. If Israel and the Diaspora were to be equal partners, they had to be equal in per capita median income, educational level and cultural, scientific and technical achievements.

In many of these areas, Diaspora Jewry was superior. The median per capita income of American Jewry was triple that of Israel. One third of the Israeli population was below the poverty level and only one third of Israel's adult population earned enough to pay income tax. Only 56% of Israel's adult population (18-65) was in the work force (the lowest percentage in the developed world). Over 90% of American Jewry's young people attended university as opposed to only 30% of Israel's young people. The status of women in the West was significantly higher than in Israel – especially amongst Diaspora Jews. Standards of public administration and governance not to mention religious pluralism in most of the host countries of Diaspora Jewry were higher than those in Israel. It was evident that the partnership could not succeed with a super-developed Diaspora interacting with a semi-developed Israel. If the purpose of Zionism was to serve the Jewish People then it was apparent that despite its earlier monumental achievements, Israel was not up to the task in the 21st century.

The aim of the *Upgrade Israel Project* was to make Israel the showcase of the entire Jewish People, the practical instrument of Jewish idealism and energy. A central task of the Diaspora was to help Israel achieve this aim.

The keystone of the upgrading project was determined to be the economy. Throughout history, economic dynamism had been the foundation of scientific and cultural vitality: from the ancient Greeks to the Moslem Caliphate to the European Renaissance and Enlightenment to the American Republic. The high points in Chinese and Hindu culture were also based on relative economic dynamism.

In a famous speech at the General Assembly of the United Jewish Communities in the United States in 2008, the Israeli Prime Minister put forward the notion that Israel's central goal was to become one of the most prosperous countries in the world in terms of median per capita income by 2030. During the speech he shocked his audience by stating that he intended to notify the American government that by 2010 Israel would no longer ask for any foreign aid. Israel's GNP at the time was 150 billion dollars a year. The one and a half billion dollars of Military American aid could be made up by a mere 1% economic growth in one year. He said:

> Since we must sustain a 5-7% yearly growth rate over the next 20 years in order to make Israel the most prosperous country per capita in the world, and since our economy has reached the size it has, it would be immoral, undignified and illogical, to continue to come to Uncle Sam for a handout. Moreover, this aid has become a cushion enabling us Israelis to put off the economic and managerial reforms necessary to make our country as efficient in its administration as it must become in order to achieve this goal. Self evident efficiencies in our public administration alone will cover the loss of the aid.

We must say to the American people: 'Thank you for your support and assistance in the past. And even though we no longer require your aid, the People of Israel are your abiding ally in eternal friendship and gratitude.'

The Prime Minister went on to say that he wished all Diaspora contributions to go to the *Jewish Energy Project*. He said this was the best way to leverage contributions and increase their effect and to significantly enhance Jewish security, economy and society.

In the subsequent question and answer period he responded to criticism for stressing economics over social and cultural issues. He pointed out that to achieve this aim Israel would have to: close the social-ethnic gap, integrate the ultra-Orthodox and the Arabs into Israel's knowledge economy and upgrade the status of women across various sectors. Social justice, he said, would be the inevitable consequence of such a policy.

In response to another objection that aid and contributions were still very helpful to the Israeli economy, even if no longer vital, he said that economics is not a zero sum quantitative enterprise. It is based on cultural values and characteristics which derive from the psychology of a society. Imagine the pride, and energy resulting from Israel becoming economically Bar Mitzvah. Imagine the economic dynamism that would be an end result of this. He predicted that this step will be the economic equivalent of 'less is more' – less external aid, more economic dynamism. From the perspective of 2020 we see that this prediction was accurate.

HOW THIS WAS ACHIEVED

It became a national aim to make Israel's civil service and public administration the most efficient in the world. "Sophisticated" commentators scoffed, calling it far-fetched. Individuals with a more historic bent and a more optimistic temperament compared it to the challenge of building the best air force in the world in the 1950's, which given the situation of the country at the time was even more far-fetched.

The two methods proposed to achieve this were the non-altruistic welfare policy and the bounty system. The non-altruistic welfare policy was intended to obligate the "more unfortunate in our society" to become "not unfortunate". This was best exemplified by a new approach to the severely handicapped and other home bound people. It was recognized that modern technology had provided us with ways to alter our perceptions. "There is no such thing as handicapped persons; there are only groups of citizens with different infrastructure needs" became the working slogan.

Technology and the end of physical work made this a reasonable slogan. Several decades previously it would have been ridiculous to make such a statement. Sophisticated technology and the end of physical work have done for *Handicapped Liberation* much the same what it did for *Women's Liberation*. The knowledge economy and the availability of the Internet enabled people to work from home and make an excellent living. Most of the work done by government clerks was administrative and did not require their presence at the workplace. Consequently, it became government policy to replace retiring government workers with homebound handicapped people who could do the same job at a distance. This saved the taxpayer money in two ways: large groups of people were taken off welfare and less money was needed to maintain offices. The infrastructure built by the government for handicapped government workers was made available to the private sector. They began utilizing these previously unused human resources to their benefit and to the benefit of society at large.

Growth promoting welfare policies, using the technologies and possibilities of globalization, were applied to other social issues: single parent families; womens' rights and opportunities; lifelong educating and credentialing etc. Ever-growing numbers of dependent, tax consuming citizens became independent, self-sufficient tax paying citizens.

Today hardly anyone is "on welfare" in the old sense of the word. The pride and self esteem of previously demoralized citizens has increased. Another consequence has been budget surpluses that have enabled both tax cuts and substantial increases in retirement benefits and education. From having one of the most disgraceful incomes in the developed world in 2006, today's Israeli Social Security recipients enjoy very comprehensive benefits. Israel's expenditures per pupil are now also amongst the highest in the world. Increased expenditures combined with efficiencies in administration released greater resources for frontline pedagogical functions, including teacher salaries and classroom conditions resulting in a much improved educational system.

The bounty system was a monetary reward to anyone who proposed a money saving suggestion to perform or replace a public service more efficiently. The reward (or bounty) was 25% of the first year's savings. Many public servants profited from this system because they knew where the inefficiencies were. They now had an incentive to become proactive in identifying them. The government workers union, instead of resisting efficiencies in the name of job security, began to conduct workshops for its members to help identify inefficiencies and write proposals on how to correct them. Public servants who eliminated their own jobs were given full pensions no matter what their age or seniority. The primary benefits of this were long term but there were also immediate savings to the tax payer as many ancillary costs were eliminated. Many former public servants pursued a second career in the private sector where their economic contribution to society was much greater.

Public administration research around the world dubbed this the "Reinvention of Israeli Bureaucracy". This became an object of international interest and groups from around the world came to Israel to study it first hand. Public expenditures in Israel as a percentage of GNP had been the highest in the developed world – over 50% as opposed to the OECD average of 41%. This has been declining 1-2% a year since the institution of the bounty system and is now 38% of GNP and still declining. Resources released by the bounty system as well as the non-altruistic welfare policy have sustained 6-8% yearly economic growth for over a decade. Job satisfaction and a feeling of wellbeing are now a common characteristic of Israeli society, in contrast to the dissatisfaction of former years.

At the time the PM announced that Israel would be doing without American aid and Diaspora contributions, the amount from both sources was less than 2% of the GNP and less than 4% of the State budget. If one subtracted the 75% of the military aid given as credits and deposited in US banks to be used to buy US equipment, the amount of both sources was less than 1% of the GNP and less than 2% of the State budget. The governmental efficiency project made up this budgetary loss in less than two years. The lost military aid was made up by freezing the deficit reduction policy for several years and gradually transferring the purchase of military equipment from the United States to Israeli companies. In 2006 the debt had been 90% of GNP and the aim had been to reduce it to 80% by 2012. Very quickly the only items Israel was buying from the US were fighter planes and some sophisticated communications and computer equipment.

The multiplier effect of this injection into Israel's military industry was such that many economists claimed that within 5 years of the declaration (i.e. in 2015) there was a substantial net benefit to the Israeli economy. The continued growth of the economy along with the efficiency project enabled Israel to renew its debt reduction policy in 2013. This year the debt has declined to 60% of GNP and by 2030 will be less than 30%.

OTHER STEPS CONTRIBUTING TO THE ECONOMY

Energy independence and growth of tourism to 10 million foreign tourists a year led to a sustained positive balance of trade and 3-4% unemployment. A lowering of taxes for hotels (as a result of public administration efficiencies) and more efficient licensing procedures for building (lowering amortization costs) enabled the hospitality sector to double wages without raising rates.

A decision was taken in 2008 to make Israel a world power in non-tangible exports: computer animation, graphics and translations (translations alone being a 25 billion dollar a year global business in 2005) were the types of businesses given special attention in business schools, the Ministry of Commerce and tax authorities. Big Diaspora donors stopped giving at the request of Israel. Instead they bought non-tangible service companies in the West and outsourced to Israel. This produced greater economic and social benefit.

Using the zip code wealth creation principle, popularized by Juan Enriques in *As the Future Catches You*, Israel instituted a policy of economic decentralization. Enriques claimed that post industrial globalization has enabled single zip codes to develop wealth equivalent to entire countries. The Kibbutz Movement adopted this principle and became pioneers once again. They re invented themselves as a high-tech and sophisticated services 'Cyber-City' with a population of 150,000. They designed their entire education system around this vision (including establishing the *Kibbutz Technological Institute*) and reinvented their ideology to conform to this vision. No more Jewish Zorbas toiling in the soil in spiritually "uplifting" physical work. Beersheba, which already had a fine university, followed suit, along with many Development Towns.

Industrial agriculture (really post industrial agriculture) was moved to an automated joint Jordanian-Israeli 'plantation' in the Arava – which became a Middle Eastern version of Imperial Valley providing the EU with inexpensive fresh vegetables year round. This enterprise was sponsored by the EU as part of a comprehensive peace initiative. Some former traditional agricultural land was still worked by boutique farmers of various sorts: olives, wine, goat cheese, organic farming etc. Most agricultural land of the kibbutz and moshav was reclaimed by nature with a corresponding enrichment of the flora and fauna of Israel. Israeli environmentalists rejoiced.

Israel began calculating international patents per million citizens as well as the number and business volume of non-tangible services export companies in order to measure economic health, and the effectiveness of the educational system. This practice has been copied by other countries and is now one of the variables cited by the *Economist* when analyzing a country.

The economy has grown by 150% relative to 2005 while the population has grown by 25%. The per capita standard of living has grown accordingly. Israel has been repeatedly cited by the World Bank as one of the top five business-friendly countries in the world – up from 26th place in 2006.

RESTRUCTURING RELATIONS WITH THE WORLD

The decline of oil neutralized the power of *Jihadists*, reactionaries and thugs. This empowered progressive Arabs and Moslems and encouraged them to advocate a *Second Caliphate* based on the knowledge economy rather than oil. Dependence on the knowledge economy obligated their respective countries to become open societies with constitutional protections and democratic institutions. This presented Israel with both an opportunity and a solution to a chronic problem. The massive influx of technical and scientific skills from the former Soviet Union in the 1990's had been a necessary feature of Israel becoming one of the world's high-tech centers. Israel's continued high-tech dynamism and the lessening of engineering and scientific aliya from the former Soviet Union had resulted in a severe shortage of technical manpower and a threat to economic growth. A substantial portion of this problem had been solved by the simple application of social justice. The Israeli Arab sector as well as a significantly higher proportion of the non-Ashkenazi Jewish sector had begun to contribute their share of engineers, scientists and technicians to the Israeli economy. But this was not enough and shortages had begun to develop.

Israeli economic policy makers decided to turn this problem into an opportunity and create projects designed to improve relations with our neighbors. The new Arab dedication to the knowledge economy was a useful backdrop to this Israeli initiative. Israeli economic parks with branches of Israeli companies were established adjacent to Egyptian and Jordanian airports to exploit their surplus technical and engineering human resources. Israeli managers flew in every morning and returned home every evening. The Tel-Aviv Cairo shuttle especially came to resemble the New York-Washington shuttle.

Egyptian officialdom, recognizing more than the rest of the Arab world, that Israel could perform the same economic tasks in the knowledge economy for the Arab world that Honk Kong did for China in the industrial economy, decided to build a Science City at *El Arish* adjacent to Israel's southern border, which was a half hour high speed train ride from Tel Aviv. This was soon compared to

Guangzhou adjacent to Hong Kong, the development of which was a major factor in China's economic reform and subsequent remarkable growth. The Egyptians received EU planning and financial support for the idea. Since the Israeli economy has already absorbed most of Jordon's manpower surplus, its future growth is tied to the Egyptian initiative – which still has vast pools of underutilized academic talent.

Not wishing to be overly dependent on Arab countries, Israel has also established a similar arrangement in the Anatolia region of Turkey – a half hour commuter flight from Tel Aviv. Israel is also exploring the possibility of similar setups in African capitals, as a magnet for underutilized African talent. Not only has this development been beneficial economically it has provided Israel with favorable PR. Israel has begun to be seen as a bridge between the developed and the developing worlds. What western "idealists" and NGOs have been preaching, Israel is doing.

During this period Israel has become an Asian economic force by continuing to upgrade relations with China and India as well as the other dynamic economies of Southeast Asia. By 2016 Asia had become the fourth leg of Israel's economic table joining in equal measure the EU, USA, and its own domestic market. This strategy was reinforced by Jewish-Hindu and Jewish-Chinese Friendship Associations in the Diaspora.

ISRAELI DEMOCRACY

Grandiose plans to totally restructure the Israeli electoral and political system yielded to a more practical and incremental approach which gradually improved the quality of Israeli democracy. Calls for a Presidential system and/or direct regional elections of the entire Knesset (to replace the list system) were dropped. It was finally recognized that in modern political history politicians had never voted for anything that would endanger their own political careers. It was further recognized that calling for such far-reaching and unachievable reforms actually inhibited the adoption of reforms that were politically possible and would enhance the system. The course taken was a conscious imitation of the English strategy of incremental constitutionalism and reform. Unlike the English strategy it did not take centuries, but rather years.

The steps taken were:

- Passage of a party primaries election law which, as in the United States, designated a particular day for all party primaries. This was regulated by the State and conducted according to criteria similar to the general elections (again as in the United States). Criminal sanctions for violating primary election laws were identical to those of the general elections. These laws were made more severe. This eliminated much corruption and established more public confidence in the process.

- Adoption of the Norwegian Law requiring all Ministers and Deputy Ministers to resign from the Knesset, their seats to be taken by candidates behind them on the party lists. This reinforced the separation of powers principle between the executive and legislative. It also reinforced effective legislative oversight. A typical Knesset had been composed of: 40 new MKs (the highest percentage of turnover in the democratic world – a function of the list system) who had little knowledge of committee work and needed time to become effective; 20 MKs serving as Ministers or Deputy Ministers with little time for committee work and with a built-in conflict of interest between their executive and legislative oversight functions; 20 MKs who were former Ministers or Deputy Ministers who many times felt themselves above the drudgery of committee work. This left a grand total of 40 MKs to perform the oversight role of the Knesset. The Norwegian Law added another 20 MKs to this function. It was also politically attractive to the rank and file of the larger parties because it enhanced the opportunity to become a MK. This political self-interest made it doable.

- Doubling the electoral threshold to 5% of the votes cast. This meant that any party with less than 5% of the votes cast would not have its candidates seated. This further increased the disincentive of very small parties to run and made it easier to form coalitions. This reduced public cynicism.

- Limiting the election campaign to 40 days from the fall of the government to elections and another 10 days to form a government. This saved up to 40 days of indecision and expense and helped lessen public disrespect for the process.

- The concluding significant law passed in this process determined that 30 Members of Knesset were to be elected from regional electoral districts. This was the only concession to direct regional elections that was possible as under the more far reaching reform proposals (calling for from 80-120 members to be directly elected in regional elections) MKs might be voting themselves out of office. This was, therefore, a politically feasible compromise. Part of the compromise determined that the 30 regionally elected MKs could not serve as Ministers or Deputy Ministers. They were elected to serve a particular constituency and this is what they were required to do. This part of the compromise was also politically attractive to MKs elected under the party list system because it increased their chances for portfolios. It was also politically attractive to rank and file party members who felt they had a better chance to become candidates in regional primaries. From the reform aspect it guaranteed an additional 30 MKs fulfilling their parliamentary oversight function. Within a decade this law and the Norwegian Law doubled the effective number of MKs performing this function.

Several other laws were passed that enhanced Israeli constitutionality and democracy. Members of party central committees were prohibited from being lobbyists and banned from being present in Knesset committees and sub-committee meetings. This was to prevent them from intimidating Members of Knesset in favor of special interests. The law against insulting government workers was revoked. It was replaced by a law against abusing citizens. This law had provisions for fining government workers whose laxity, inefficiency or hostility caused damage to a citizen's person or property.

Moreover, personal liability was placed on departmental directors of ministries and board members of governmental firms. They could now be sued by citizens for damages caused by incompetence, inefficiency or misapplication of the law. The government employees and not the taxpayers would have to pay for damages. This greatly limited the ambitions of incompetent political operatives to aspire to public jobs for which they were not qualified. The general level of public service increased greatly as a result.

Government payment practices to suppliers of goods and services had been notoriously poor – driving dozens of small and medium size businesses into bankruptcy. The immorality of these practices, as well as the economic damage they caused, was finally exposed. Binding legislation was passed into law. All government bodies (local, national and public bodies) are now required by law to pay all bills by end of month plus 30 against a pro forma invoice. Nonpayment subjected departmental directors to personal liability to the supplier. Pro forma invoices have also become legally binding in the private sector. Taxes will be paid upon receipt of payment only and after checks have cleared. As a consequence of these laws the liquidity of small and medium size companies has improved greatly and the number of bankruptcies has declined. The discipline, quality and ethics of public management have also significantly improved.

All government bodies (local, national and public) are now required by law to construct a website atlas of public employees, consultants and contractors – their names, what they do and what they are paid. This has become a useful tool of the bounty system (and "bounty hunters"). It greatly improved the public service and political ethics. It became impossible to hide unqualified hacks and inefficiencies and absurdities in the system. The argument that this violated privacy was rejected. If you are a public servant, you are employed by the public and the public has the right to know who it employs and what they are being paid. If you want to be private, you can't be public.

Contempt of court laws were amended and limited to the courtroom only. Anyone could say or write anything against a judge outside the courtroom. The principle of the limitations of power was finally applied to the courts. Israeli Bar feedback became a legal and integral part of choosing higher court judges (as it is in the United States) and it was legislated that at least one supreme court judge not be a previously seated judge but rather a practicing lawyer or academic. All this was reflected in a change of attitude towards the public by politicians and public servants, which was demonstrated by a landmark speech in the Knesset by a new Speaker:

> We must realize that mistrust in government is inherently healthy in a democracy and even a necessity if we are to widen and deepen the constitutional protections we all value. The higher the automatic trust in government, the easier it is for totalitarian tendencies to emerge. This kind of trust enables shrewd demagogues to create a tyranny of the mob. In the United States in the 50's trust in the government was at its highest – so was McCarthyism. The growing wariness of the Israeli citizenry to public officials (elected and civil servants) is not a sign of the decline of democracy; it is a sign of the maturity of democracy. It is not a sign of a decline

in the objective morals or abilities of the government apparatus but a reflection of the rising expectations of the citizenry. The moral and administrative levels of Israel's public servants might be higher than in the 50's but the demands of the citizens are higher still. The rising expectations of a free people are the greatest guarantee of freedom. Let us all dread the day when our people are happy with us!

| CHAPTER 14 |

THE TRIUMPH OF JEWISH HASBARA

A major turning point in modern Jewish history was the recognition that Israel's war was *Grand Strategic* and involved the entire Jewish People. Grand Strategy refers to economic, political, social and public relations resources as well as military. Chapters 11, 12, and 13 have dealt primarily with the economic, political and social aspects of the struggle. This chapter will deal primarily with public relations, or as we say in Hebrew *Hasbara*.

FROM EXPLANATION TO INFORMATION

Israel's information campaign or lack thereof had long been a focal point of Jewish debate. Part of the problem is that the Hebrew word for information – *Hasbara* – literally means explanation and not information. Explanation is to information what sales are to marketing. Nothing had been more counterproductive than Israeli "experts" in communications appearing on television and "explaining" the value of their Israeli 'product' and the essential weaknesses of the Arab 'competition' when Israel had not been 'marketed' properly for decades

Before the Six Day War Israel had enjoyed a tremendous *Hasbara* advantage for positive and negative reasons. The post Holocaust "phoenix rising from the ashes" metaphor of a nation crushed like no other nation had ever been crushed taking hold of its destiny and building a progressive modern country in a barren land in the face of constant hostility against overwhelming odds excited the imagination of Europe and America, as well as large segments of the Third World – especially Africa.

The social experiments of kibbutz, moshav, and large scale cooperatives excited the imagination of Europe's democratic Left and gave this tiny country a special status in the *Socialist International*. Golda Meir's standing in the *International* was almost equivalent to that of Willy Brandt and Harold Wilson. Israel's comprehensive Trade Unionism (90% of the working population during its early years) gave Israel a disproportionate weight in international Trade Unionism. All this attracted "progressive" public opinion.

It also provided Diaspora Jewry with a source of pride and earned Gentile admiration. Israel was easy to sell. Sympathetic Jews and Gentile anti anti-Semites dominated the campuses and media. The best selling book *Exodus* and movies such as *Exodus* and *Cast a Giant Shadow* were public relations boons that could not be bought for billions of dollars today.

The competition was easy to disparage. King Saud's gold plated Cadillac and dozens of wives were objects of parody and ridicule in popular culture, from stand up comedians to James Bond movies. Nasser and others came across as pro-Soviet dupes or thugs. The price of oil was low and dependence on Middle Eastern oil was still marginal. Few Arab or Moslem students and fewer Moslem faculty members were on western campuses.

Following the Six Day War the Arabs began to engage in marketing on a major scale. They focused on the centers of future public opinion making – the university campuses. This was a turning point in the Arab-Israeli conflict. This was the first time in their struggle with Zionism that the Arabs adopted a *future* oriented strategy that would bear fruit after several decades.

Zionism had been the ultimate future oriented political movement up until the Six Day War. Following the first Zionist Congress in Basle in 1897 Herzl had written that he had created the Jewish State, perhaps not in a year or in ten years but certainly in 50 years. In 1947 the United Nations accepted the *Partition Plan*. Herzl's *The Jewish State* was a futurist tract and his book *Old New Land* was a futurist scenario.

Ben Gurion was the embodiment of a Jewish futurist (the next 1,000 years being more important than the last 1,000 years). His call that Israel strive to become a *light unto the nations* was recognition that unless Israel became a light unto the nations it would not be a light unto the Jews. Without a transcendent *future* vision the Zionist project would ultimately fail.

Labor Zionism, in its many manifestations, was preoccupied with creating the future Jewish utopia. The writings of Labor Zionism's great opponent Jabotinsky were also characterized by a stress on the future. His historical works were educational analogies intended to inspire future action. What separated modern religious Zionists from the ultra-Orthodox was their affiliation with Labor Zionism and its stress on the future. This future orientation had given us a tremendous cultural and political advantage over the Arabs.

Following the Six Day War "practical" native born Israelis became a dominant force in Israeli politics. They disdained grand visions of the future and preoccupied themselves with the immediate. Their nickname in popular jargon was the 'implementers' – *bitzuistim*. Moshe Dayan was the foremost example of this generation. Following the Yom Kippur War the barrenness (and ultimate inefficiency) of a visionless Zionism was strongly felt. But the vacuum was filled by visions of the past, not the future. The settlement project of *Gush Emunim* in the occupied territories co-opted both the idealism and the instruments of the early Zionist pioneers. They claimed they were continuers of the early pioneers and the true representatives of Zionism. Unfortunately, many in Israel and in the West believed them. If this was "authentic Zionism" then perhaps Zionism itself was wrong. The seeds of post-Zionism in Israel and resurgent anti-Zionism in the West were planted. If *Gush Emunim* was the poster child of Zionism (and they did provide the best photo opportunities for a visual communications ruled planet) then how could "explainers" sell our message to a West ruled by post-colonial guilt?

The difference between *Gush Emunim* and the early pioneers was self evident. *Gush Emunim* wished to reconstruct the past at the expense of the future whilst the early pioneers had used the past as an inspiration to build a better future. But Labor and Liberal Zionist parties had no real response to *Gush Emunim*. They had no updated future oriented Zionist vision to offer. All they could do was fall back on their past achievements. This just helped *Gush Emunim* who acknowledged and praised past Labor achievements but portrayed themselves as continuers of the pioneering legacy. The revival of future Zionist visions – described in chapters 11-13 – finally offered a Zionist alternative to *Gush Emunim*; an alternative that rejuvenated Jewish idealism and Gentile admiration. Israeli *Hasbara* once again had a marketable product.

ISLAMIZATION OF THE WEST

Large scale Moslem immigration to the West coincided with the decline of Israeli *Hasbara*. In 1950 Western Europe had less than a quarter of a million Moslems and two million Jews. In 2006 it had 20 million Moslems and one and a half million Jews. In 1950 North America had almost no Moslems. By 2006 Canada had more Moslems than Jews and the number of Moslems in the United States was about to surpass the Jews.

Following the Six Day War great numbers of Arab students, financed by oil money scholarships, poured onto western campuses. They were well schooled in focused, on-message propaganda. Financed by their home countries, few had to work while studying. Their full time extra-curricular activity was pro-Arab and anti-Israel propaganda. It often seemed that the price of their scholarship was to become fulltime propagandists. Oil prices and western dependence on Moslem oil increased significantly during this period, further complicating the picture.

Europe was initially an easier market for Arab propagandists to penetrate than the United States. The post-colonial mindset of guilt ridden Europeans and their loss of moral self assurance (ironically to a large extent because of the Holocaust) made Europeans easy targets for Arab propagandists.

Unfortunately, Israel's own behavior helped the Arabs. The Israeli occupation (and the early stages of "colonial" settlements) coincided with the beginning of the special relationship with the United States which was bogged down in Vietnam. This occurred during the height of the student revolutions of the 60's. The timing could not have been worse.

For politically correct public opinion, Israel had become a "militaristic colonial aggressor, an ally of anti-Third World neo-imperialist America". The Arabs, especially the Palestinians, were an oppressed and exploited Third World people. It was self-evident what position "progressive" people would take.

The special relationship Israel had enjoyed with European progressives began to wane. To be an academic with a "mature" view of world affairs one had to disabuse oneself of naïve support for Israel. Sentimental sympathy with previously oppressed Jews was not mature. Now they are the oppressors. In any case Zionism and Jewry are not one and the same. One could be an anti-Zionist without being anti-Jewish. There was no lack of Jewish "intellectuals" who, in order to be politically correct and transcend their own ethnic provinciality, gave credence to this distinction. American academia, looking over its shoulder at Europe in order to be "sophisticated" followed suit.

Jewish and Israeli students were overwhelmed by this wave of sudden hostility, while the self-confident and somewhat arrogant post Six Day War Israeli establishment was dismissive of the threat and provided no guidance. Campuses and the media were seen as marginal to the centers of real power that "manly" Israeli politicians were cultivating. Intellectuals and political commentators who were disturbed by developments were treated with condescension and disdain. Their concern for what the *goyim* were thinking was dismissed as a lingering characteristic of the ghetto Jew. There was something effeminate and "old Jew" about this kind of worrying. Manly "new Jews" concerned themselves with real problems, not with words. They used a misinterpretation of Ben Gurion's famous statement: "It's not important what the *goyim* think (or say); it's important what the Jews do".

In truth there hadn't been an Israeli leader who had been more concerned with what the *goyim* thought than Ben Gurion. This was because the *goyim* sometimes acted on what they thought and what they *did* was important to the Jews. Ben Gurion never ignored or dismissed Gentile views. He always wanted to know what the *goyim* were thinking. But he also knew that no matter what they thought we still had the freedom to do something – *something not anything*.

Geopolitical constraints were Ben Gurion's forte and what made him a great leader. He was for the U.N. *Partition Plan* and fought for it against substantial Zionist opposition because he knew it was what was obtainable given the political limitations of the time. He also knew it was a window of opportunity that would close as political reality began to work against us. He would never have uttered those infamous post Six Day War words "time is on our side". For him time was never on our side.

There was, therefore, no coherent, organized, 'on message' Jewish response to the Arab propaganda machine. A hundred Arab spokesmen would use the same arguments and have the same responses. Fifty Jewish spokesmen would have fifty different responses. Israel's previous public relations advantage had been unplanned. It had been realized inadvertently – by Israel's own achievements, by the corrupt state of the Arab world and by Hollywood.

Moreover, the occupation and the beginnings of the settlement project splintered Israeli public opinion and Israeli political parties into many shades of opinion. From Herut's 'annex everything' to Mapam's 'give everything back' to Labor having a half a dozen positions within the same party. When public opinion is conflicted a democracy has difficulty in formulating and executing a coherent information campaign. What product were we selling? Israel the colonial power exploiting cheap Arab labor or Israel the peace seeker and beacon of social justice? What policy were we explaining? Our historic rights to the land; our territorial requirements for security; our desire for peace; our need for cheap labor; our own inability to decide what we want?

Being the only democracy in the Middle East we could not design or control our message when it came to the occupation. Our message was as conflicted as our internal politics. Thus steps taken to rid ourselves of the occupation became Israel's greatest *Hasbara* achievement.

NEGATIVE AND POSITIVE HASBARA

The revamped Jewish *Hasbara* campaign of 2008 had two aspects: negative and positive. Negative *Hasbara* aimed at *de-legitimizing*

Arab/Moslem and certain NGO and media positions vis-à-vis Israel, Zionism and the Jews. Positive *Hasbara* was based on Israel's achievements. Tactics were new. They included websites, Google ads, email chain letters and articles, specialty magazines, blogs, exposé books etc.

The strategy of weakening Persian Gulf oil power also paid dividends in the new *Hasbara* campaign. With less oil money being contributed to universities, dozens of spurious *Middle East Studies Programs* (dedicated to turning out anti-Israel partisans rather than objective scholars) were enfeebled or transformed into legitimate academic enterprises. Less oil money also limited the dissemination of anti-Semitic and anti-Israel literature as well as negative public relations. The oil states had to sell off substantial foreign investments in order to finance the daily activities of their countries. Their influence over the international investment community and media lessened. The beginning of their integration into the knowledge economy and the kind of leadership and international partnerships this required also served to moderate their position. It was harder for them to explain and more difficult for western apologists to excuse their blatant anti-Semitism.

The relative power of international oil companies (which were indirect partners in Arab PR and lobbying) declined. The relative power of international high tech companies with a significant Israeli presence continued to grow. Israel's own high tech powerhouse and its developments in information technology, alternate energy, materials science, medical technology, bio-tech and nano-tech continued to make image enhancing headlines.

Practical peace making with the Palestinians was the ultimate positive *Hasbara*. It revealed that the root cause of instability in the Middle East was not the Israel/Palestine issue. The *true* "root cause" reflected the title of a controversial book *The Crisis of Islamic*

Civilization: the Cultural Origins of Jihadism (2010). As the book was written by Moslem intellectuals the academic left could not dismiss it as racist as they had done with Samuel Huntingdon's *Clash of Civilizations*, (Touchstone, 1998) The book was modeled on the classic *The Crisis of German Ideology: Intellectual Origins of the Third Reich* (Howard Fertig Publishers, 1999) by Prof. George Mosse. It was analogous to Mosse's critical analysis of German cultural pathologies prior and parallel to the rise of Hitler.

The Crisis of Islamic Civilization asserted that certain psychological pathologies in Islamic culture, a result of not having been able to integrate into modernity, were the primary cause of the social and political pathologies affecting Islamic societies. Much of the analysis was based on Bernhard Lewis's book *What Went Wrong* (Weidenfield and Nicolson, 2002), which was an historical investigation of Islam's failure to deal with modernity. One particular portion of *The Crisis of Islamic Civilization* stands out and sums up the thrust of the book:

> For every Moslem killed by Israelis, British and Americans since 1950 a hundred Moslems have been killed by our fellow Moslems. 50,000 gassed in Yemen by Nasser in the 60's, a million killed in the Iran-Iraq war in the 80's; 200,000 killed in Algeria in the 90's; Saddam Hussein's slaughter of his own citizens; tens of thousands killed in sectarian Sunni-Shia strife in Pakistan and Iraq. Over 8 million Moslems have been killed by our fellow Moslems in this period, compared to 60,000 by Israel (mostly on the battlefield).
>
> Compared to unsubstantiated western contempt for Islamic culture, real internal Moslem contempt is striking. This intra-Moslem contempt is exemplified by Wahabi Sunnis destroying Shia shrines in Saudi Arabia.
>
> Moslem contempt for non-Moslems has been even more prominent. Moslem Sudan murdered over one million non-Moslems in southern Sudan. Moslem Taliban committed the greatest cultural atrocity of the 21st century when it blew up Buddhist statues, which were one of the wonders of the world. This aroused no Moslem

indignation, but caricatures in a Danish newspaper moved millions to demonstrate, riot and boycott.

Our culture of self-pity and denial as well as our inability to engage in constructive self-criticism are the true enemies of Islam. *The Moslems themselves are the greatest enemy of Islam, not the Zionists, the Americans or the British.*

The book was attacked by Moslem and multi-cultural apologists as a self-hating caricature. They held to the view that if not for the invasion of Zionism Islam would have had wonderful relations with the West. The Palestinian-Israeli peace, however, removed this excuse for failed Islamic states. As was to be expected, the radical Left (especially the Jewish subsection of it) and radical Islamists did not accept this "false peace" and continued to attack Israel. But these positions were becoming 'curiouser and curiouser' in the eyes of public opinion. One of the tangential benefits of the peace was a significant marginalization of the advocates of bizarre political belief.

NEGATIVE HASBARA

Grants were provided to Black intellectuals and academics to research the Arab slave trade, which preceded and outlasted the European slave trade. High powered PR turned a book entitled *The Arab Slave Trade* (2009) into a best seller. The following quote reflects its theme: "The Arab Slave Trade lasted from 700 to 1911 AD. It has been estimated that 14 million slaves were sold and that 14-20 million African men, women and children died throughout this period". Another best selling book was entitled *Arab Oil Politics and Africa* (2010). This book demonstrated how Arab oil politics, especially the boycotts of the 1970's had contributed to Africa's economic misery.

One academic monograph in particular had a tremendous impact on African intellectuals. *Cultural Imperialism and its Impact on*

Modernization in Africa (2011) was an objective analysis of European and Islamic cultures as foreign implants in Africa and their relative impact on Africa's attempts to modernize. Statistical comparisons of the economic and social development of Christian and Moslem areas of Africa were not favorable to Islam. Qualitative comparisons regarding the status of women and attitudes towards secular education produced even more negative results. The consequences of Islamic missionary success in Africa and Christian missionary success in China were also compared. One of the controversial conclusions of the book was that the biggest impediment to African development in the 21st century was not the legacy of European imperialism, nor the neo-colonialism of international corporations. It was rather the inertia of certain African cultural practices combined with certain Islamic cultural attitudes.

These publications coincided with the rise of new technocratic African elites interested in development rather than utopian ideologies. They were concerned more with the welfare of their people than conforming to political fashion. These developments were favorable to Israel and enabled the regeneration of African-Israeli relations that were so notable before the 6 Day War. Israel was again seen as an alternative model for development – even by moderate African Moslems. African countries no longer automatically sided with their Arab and Moslem colleagues in the United Nations and other international bodies against Israel. Sentimental identification with the Arab cause was neutralized. This, and practical developmental considerations, made African elites and African-American intellectuals more predisposed to Israel and to Jewish issues. General public opinion soon followed. The balanced African approach to the Middle East helped neutralize hostile "progressive" European opinion. Simplistic slogans treating the Third World as if it were a single entity went out of fashion. Progressive thinking once again became as sophisticated and nuanced as it had been prior to the rise of the postmodern Left.

A series of exposé books and television programs dealing with the Palestinians were produced. *A History of the Palestinians* (2009) included statistics about the hugely disproportionate aid they had received compared to other refugee problems following WWII. Another comparison demonstrated how by 2006 the Palestinians had received four times the aid per individual that Europe had received under the Marshall Plan. A particularly revealing chapter dealt with how UNRWA bureaucrats helped Palestinian politicians misrepresent demographics in order to get more money from the international community. UNRWA was revealed to have become a corrupt, inefficient, self-serving and self-perpetuating bureaucracy that had a vested interest in preserving Palestinian suffering.

Another book taking the same line was *The Enemy is Us: a Critical View of the Palestinian Problem* (2010). It dealt with the harm done to the Palestinians as a result of the forgiving attitudes of the international community.

There was also *Palestinian Refugees: the Great Hoax* (2009) which compared the per capita aid given to other refugees (in Africa and the refugees of the India Partition tragedy in particular). Finally a public debate began on how the disproportionate preoccupation with the Palestinian problem and Israel bashing had diverted attention from other humanitarian crises. One prominent study compared the airtime and print space given to the Palestinians and the Lebanese war from 2004 to 2006 with that given to the genocide in the Darfur region of Sudan during the same period.

Injustices to the Palestinians were not denied or dismissed. But it was no longer taboo to point out that past injustices did not release a nation's leaders from making rational policy decisions based on the constraints of political reality. Arafat's rebuff of Barak at Camp David for fear of his own people was compared to Ben Gurion's fearless acceptance of the *Partition Plan* and his battle to sell it to a hostile Zionist leadership and Jewish public opinion.

A legal academic monograph became the subject of debate amongst professional jurists and international NGOs. It was commissioned by *The International Association of Jewish Lawyers and Jurists* www.intjewishlawyers.org, its affiliate *The American Association of Jewish Lawyers and Jurists* www.jewishlawyers.org and *The North American Network of Jewish Lawyers' Organizations* www.nanjlo.org. It was entitled *Does the U.N.'s Treatment of Israel and Certain Consequences and Interpretations of this Treatment Constitute an Accumulative and Ongoing 'Bill of Attainder' and Violation of Constitutional Principles?* (2009)

Bills of Attainder are laws especially designed to impose legal sanctions or disabilities on a particular individual or class of people. They have been unconstitutional in the Anglo Saxon legal tradition since the Magna Carta and are specifically banned in the English Bill of Rights and in the American Constitution.

The contemporary interpretation of UN General Assembly Resolution 194 calling for the return of Palestinian refugees to their former homes in Israel was cited as a prime example of a *Bill of Attainder*. No similar resolution existed for the 20 million refugees of the Indian partition or for the 9 million ethnic Germans expelled from their ancestral homelands in Eastern Europe following WWII. Moreover, implementation of 194 (as *interpreted* by Israel's enemies) would have meant the destruction of the Jewish State. This would have been a violation of the UN Charter declaring the right of every People to self determination.

The Palestinians could have achieved self-determination without the 'right of return' to Israel. Implementation of this "right" would have deprived the Jews of their right of self-determination. It was thus unconstitutional on two grounds: it was a *Bill of Attainder* the implementation of which would have resulted in the death of a sovereign state and it would have violated the UN Charter.

A broader debate ensued. Is international governance majoritarian or constitutional? Are the rights of states, nations and peoples to life, liberty and a land of their own inalienable, constitutionally guaranteed and indifferent to majority whim, or are they dependent on the will and agreement of the majority? *The question was asked, would African Americans have achieved their full civil rights if the American system had been majoritarian and not constitutional?*

NGOs were another target of negative *Hasbara* with the express purpose of putting them on the defensive in all things related to Jewish issues. The International Committee of the Red Cross (ICRC) was one example. They had had knowledge of the Holocaust and declined to publicize it to the world claiming that international law forbade them to do it. This was especially incongruous as the ICRC had since often accused Israel of violating International Law. The ICRC did not protest when the Swiss State refused to give refuge to Jews fleeing Nazi Germany. The Swiss sent them back to certain death in Germany. It was not well known at the time that the ICRC was a statutory body of Switzerland. The Red Cross flag and the Swiss flag are the same. The Red Cross sent Swiss physicians to treat Nazi troops on the Eastern front and some ICRC officials aided Nazis to flee to South America after the war.

The ICRC hired Francois Genoud, a notorious Swiss Nazi, to work for them in Belgium after the Holocaust. To see how sordid this individual was, access the following from *Hitler's Swiss Connection,* by David Preston (*Philadelphia Inquirer* Jan.1997) http://members. aol.com/voyl/barbie/genoud.htm. These little known facts were now widely publicized. A scholarly book by Jean-Claude Favez (*The Red Cross and the Holocaust,* Cambridge University Press, 1999) was reissued. As a consequence of this publicity the ICRC became wary of their criticism of Israel, to the benefit of Jewish *Hasbara*.

A yearly *Arithmetic of Tears* report was issued. It added up the airtime and print space devoted to various crises around the world in relation to the number of dying or suffering in these same crises. It took particular notice of the reports of *Amnesty International* and *Human Rights Watch*. A survey reviewing twenty years of Amnesty reports (between 1986-2006) added up the print space devoted to Rwanda, Darfur, and human rights in the Moslem world and compared it to the print space devoted to Israel and Palestine – *without comment*. Funding of these and other advocate organizations was also noted and publicized as well as the political biographies of its activists – also *without comment*. Israeli and Jewish spokesmen when asked about the report replied '*no comment*'. The silence was deafening. The facts spoke for themselves. Israel ceased to be the object of sanctimonious condescension. Criticism of Israel became to the point and often on target.

For example, when *Amnesty* condemned Israel for its treatment of foreign workers and its poor record in stopping the trafficking in women for the sex trade, decent Israelis applauded and thanked them. This had been a disgrace and an affront to Ben Gurion's vision, not to mention to Jewish tradition. When *Amnesty* ceased its disproportionate Israel bashing it began to fulfill its proper role as an international oversight organization on human rights. Israel benefited all around.

A similar development occurred with *Human Rights Watch*. They evolved into a professional organization not dominated by activists with a political agenda. They had been particularly embarrassed by a television program criticizing the ethics of the media in the era of cable television. The title of the program was: *When are Journalistic Ignorance and Unprofessionalism Unethical?* It related to journalists reporting on issues of which they had no knowledge. It gave examples of prejudicial statements, questions and out of context photo shots. It gave examples of journalists ignorant of facts. This type of reporting was branded unethical because, in the electronic age, pictures are iconic and poor reporting has a strategic impact that can help destroy a people.

POSITIVE HASBARA

A major issue addressed by Israel and the Diaspora was the environment. *The Jewish Global Environmental Network (JGEN)* www.jgenisrael.org along with *The Coalition on the Environment and Jewish Life* www.coejl.org, *The Heschel Center for Environmental Learning and Leadership* www.heschel.org.il, *Israel Union for Environmental Defense* www.iued.org.il , and *The Green Environment Fund (GEF)* www.gef.org.il joined to establish *Project Pristine* – dedicated to returning the Israeli environment to its original pristine condition. This project not only excited the idealism of unaffiliated Jewish youth, it also earned a great deal of positive *Hasbara*.

Between 2008 and 2015 the project turned Israel into a model for environmental responsibility. The project combined revolutions in agricultural and industrial recycling with alternative energy. Its focus was to turn Israel's human habitation into a closed system, to achieve 100% recycling of organic and industrial waste. *Project Pristine* overlapped with the *Israel Energy Project* discussed in chapter 12.

Israel is a major bird migration route. Half a billion birds a year migrate over Israel. Bird watching is the third most popular hobby in the world after gardening and walking. Over 50 million people worldwide engage in this hobby and are of a class of people that help determine public opinion. Half a million birdwatcher tourists visit Israel each year. *Project Pristine* publishes a multi-lingual magazine called *The Israeli Bird Watcher*. It has over ten million subscribers.

An online multi-lingual version of the magazine gets several hundred million hits a year. Israel's efforts in this aspect of conservation have earned it tens of millions of friends around the world who are an asset in its *Hasbara* campaign.

Other positive *Hasbara* resources were Israel's non-altruistic welfare policy, especially Israel's success at integrating the handicapped into society and the economy. Israeli agricultural systems and developments in water engineering and management were at the forefront of ending world hunger. The killer application was Israel's development of plants that could be directly irrigated by sea water.

The canard that Zionism was a colonialist movement was addressed in a essay entitled *The Differences between Zionism and Colonialism* (2008). It made the following points:

1. All other colonial enterprises represented or derived from an *existing* mother country or group of countries,
2. No other colonial enterprise viewed itself as *returning to its homeland,*
3. No other *modern* colonial enterprise was driven by the desire of the colonizers to escape persecution and discrimination,
4. No other colonial enterprise viewed its colonial ambition as being part and parcel of their *national* cultural, psychological and moral renewal,
5. No other colonial enterprise satisfied itself with only one colony,
6. No other colonial enterprise desired so passionately to settle a land *devoid* of natural resources,
7. No other colonial enterprise desired to create an independent state (all the others saw themselves as dependent colonies of the mother country),
8. No other colonial enterprise desired to create an entirely new society.

CONCLUSION

As a consequence of the above the special relationship the Arabs had enjoyed with western progressives for the forty years between 1967 and 2007 began to wane. To have a mature view of world affairs one had to disabuse oneself of naïve support for the Palestinians in particular and the Arabs in general. Gender apartheid in the Moslem world became an international issue, one that pro-Arab intellectuals could not explain away or justify in the name of the Palestinian issue (the famous "root cause" of everything dreadful in the Moslem world). Sentimental sympathy with previously oppressed Palestinians eroded after the Israeli-Palestinian understandings (which turned out to be Israel's greatest *Hasbara* achievement). Automatic sympathy with the Arabs was no longer mature. Now they are the oppressors – of women, of minorities and of other Moslems. For most of western public opinion events in the Middle East became a non-issue because of energy independence that helped neutralize *Jihadist* terror and the eventual peace between Israel and most of its Arab neighbors.

| CHAPTER 15 |

PRACTICAL PEACEMAKING

In 2007 practical peacemaking as a process replaced the uncompromising search for a final peace agreement. The art of the possible replaced the desire for the perfect. The Islamic concept of *Hudna* played a vital role. It enabled both sides to moderate their tactics without requiring them to forgo their ideologies. A 10 year *Hudna* between the Israelis and the Palestinians was declared.

Hudna is an Arabic term indicating 'truce' or 'armistice'. It derives from a verb root meaning 'calm'. Israelis had been suspicious of previous proposals for *Hudnas* given its place in Islamic doctrine and history. Islamic doctrine dictates that *Hudnas* with non-Moslems should be limited to ten years and should only be agreed upon if the Moslems are weak. Its purpose is to provide time to rebuild strength in order to renew the conflict with non-Moslem enemies after the ten year period. Historically the Arabs had often made use of this device. The Israelis regarded the suggestion as a cynical ploy by a weakened Palestinian resistance to gain time, rearm and resume the struggle at the time of their choosing. Israeli suspicions were legitimate as many on the Palestinian side did have deceitful intentions.

But Israeli belief in a final peace with the Palestinians had been waning while support for an interim agreement that would provide peace and quiet (in lieu of real peace) had been rising. The idea of the *Hudna* no longer seemed unappealing. This was reinforced by an historical analysis that moderated Israeli public opinion. A best case scenario would set the stage for an eventual peace. But even a worst case scenario – in which the Palestinians resumed hostilities after 10 years – would still have benefited Israel. It would have provided ten years of relative quiet, enabling development that would have increased Israel's advantage over its enemies. This had been the historical pattern.

In the 60 years of its existence every period of relative calm was better used by Israel than the Arabs. The gap in the relative strength of both sides always grew to the benefit of Israel. In the period 1948-1956 (the year of the Sinai War) Israel absorbed over a million immigrants, organized a regular and reserve army and grew its economy by 9% a year. In the period 1957-1965 Israel built one of the best armies and air forces in the world, grew its economy an average of 9% a year and absorbed hundreds of thousands of immigrants.

The period of 1967-1973 also enabled robust economic growth, significant *aliya* from the West (for the first time) as well as the upgrading of relations with American Jewry and the United States. The period of 1991 (Madrid conference) to 2000 (2nd Intifada) enabled 4-5% yearly economic growth which is substantial for a mature economy. This facilitated the absorption of over a million highly educated immigrants and the transformation of Israel into a high-tech power house (Silicon Wadi). It was also a major factor in the normalization of relations with the future super powers of China and India and the reestablishment of normal diplomatic and economic ties with Africa. It helped strengthen scientific and economic ties with the European Union and the United States and triggered peace with Jordan as well as economic ties with some Persian Gulf and North African States.

The Oslo Accords have come to be seen – post facto – as a *Hudna*. Perhaps if they had been sold as such at the outset rather than as the harbinger of a New Middle East, a great deal of disappointment and cynicism might have been avoided. With the perspective of hindsight we see that for the Zionist project the Oslo Accords were an achievement and not a mistake. Given all this, it was generally agreed that even a worst case scenario would leave Israel in better economic and security shape than its enemies.

The previous several decades of world history reinforced this view. Democratic, free-market countries with solid constitutional protections and mature technological and scientific foundations had been able to take better advantage of the global economy than totalitarian, theocratic or autocratic countries. Over any given period of time the gap between open and closed societies has been widening at an increasing rate. Since economic and scientific power is the underpinning of military power the Israeli public realized they would be better off regardless of the outcome of the *Hudna*.

AMELIORATION

But the worst case scenario did not occur. The reason being that during this ten year *Hudna* the Palestinians were forced by external and internal pressures to concentrate on development. The donor countries became more stringent in supervising the use of their money and insisting it be used for development rather than corruption. The majority of ordinary Palestinians had become sick of corruption, violence and poverty. They became outspoken in insisting that their leaders provide them with a better life. These pressures did not stop the smuggling of arms. Nor did they end Islamic dreams of eliminating the Jewish state. They did not bring about the immediate cessation of Kassam rocket fire from Gaza into Israeli population centers. What they did was to begin to bring Palestinian leadership identified with economic and social development to the foreground and begin to push leadership identified with armed struggle and dreams of an Islamic state in greater Palestine into the background.

The inertia of development began an historical process of marginalizing advocates of violence. Discreet pressure from the European Union helped eliminate racist incitement in the Palestinian educational system and media. More importantly, the EU exerted pressure to amend the *Hamas Covenant* of 1988. The Europeans finally recognized that the ideology and mass psychology underlying the *Covenant* had become the greatest obstacle to peace – greater even than the occupation. In Israel, the ideology and mass psychology of the occupation had been eroding since the 2005 disengagement from the Gaza Strip while the *Hamas* worldview had penetrated the very soul of the Palestinian psyche. Even those European leaders and opinion makers most hostile to Israel and dismissive of the substantive importance of the *Covenant* could not deny its psychological implications vis-à-vis Jewish public opinion and how this would limit flexibility on the Israeli side.

The *Covenant* maintained that the notorious anti-Semitic forgery, *The Protocols of the Elders of Zion*, was authentic and called for the extermination of Israel and the creation of a greater Islamic state in Palestine. It called all Arabs and Moslems that did not adhere to this position, traitors to Allah and implied they were deserving of death. Article 22 was especially embarrassing to the apologists for the Palestinian cause. It revealed the anti-Semitism at the heart of the Palestinian national movement. There was no way it could be interpreted as anti-Zionism. It contained every canard against the Jews in the canon of anti-Semitism:

> With their money, they took control of the world media, news agencies, the press, publishing houses, broadcasting stations, and others. With their money they stirred revolutions in various parts of the world with the purpose of achieving their interests and reaping

the fruit therein. They were behind the French Revolution, the Communist Revolution and most of the revolutions we heard and hear about... With their money they formed secret societies, such as Freemasons, Rotary Clubs, the Lions and others in different parts of the world for the purpose of sabotaging societies and achieving Zionist interests. With their money they were able to control imperialistic countries and instigate them to colonize many countries in order to enable them to exploit their resources and spread corruption there...They were behind World War I, when they were able to destroy the Islamic Caliphate, making financial gains and controlling resources. They obtained the Balfour Declaration, formed the League of Nations through which they could rule the world. They were behind World War II, through which they made huge financial gains by trading in armaments, and paved the way for the establishment of their state. It was they who instigated the replacement of the League of Nations with the United Nations and the Security Council to enable them to rule the world through them. There is no war going on anywhere, without having their finger in it.

Article 28 contains a lie that Goebbels would have been proud of:

We should not forget to remind every Moslem that when the Jews conquered the Holy City in 1967, they stood on the threshold of the Aqsa Mosque and proclaimed that "Mohammed is dead, and his descendants are all women"...Israel, Judaism and Jews challenge Islam and the Moslem people. "May the cowards never sleep!"

Examples of the Koranic origins of Moslem anti-Semitism were also contained in the body of the Covenant. For example Article 7 contained the following:

The Prophet, Allah, bless him and grant him salvation, has said: "The Day of Judgment will not come about until Moslems fight the Jews (killing the Jews), when the Jew will hide behind stones and trees. The stones and trees will say O Moslems, O Abdulla, there is a Jew behind me, come and kill him..."

Western countries and moderate Arab and Moslem leaders realized that these views as well as the situation on the ground had to be transformed and that different regional background music had to be created to enable progress on the peace front. Moral absolutes were relegated to the sidelines, particularly because the moral absolutes of Islam could not tolerate any semblance of Jewish autonomy. Nor could they tolerate the peace process. As article 13 of the Hamas Covenant says:

> Initiatives, and so-called peaceful solutions and international conferences, are in contradiction to the principles of the Islamic Resistance Movement...There is no solution for the Palestinian question except through Jihad. Initiatives, proposals and international conferences are all a waste of time and vain endeavors.

To counteract this implacable attitude, practical steps were formulated designed to create a situation that might eventually enable peace. At the most basic level this moderated the obsessive sanctimonious moralizing at Israel as well as the cessation of the endless stream of hostile United Nations resolutions. It was finally realized that all this did was make the job of the advocates of peace in Israel more difficult.

DEFUSING THE PALESTINIAN PROBLEM

One of the reasons the 2000 Camp David talks broke down was the issue of the Palestinian refugees. The Palestinian leadership claimed the *right of return* to Israel according to their interpretation of United Nations General Assembly resolution 194. Israel countered that this would mean the destruction of the Jewish State and of Jewish self-determination. Since self-determination is defined as a right in the United Nations Charter this interpretation of resolution

194 was, in Israel's eyes, in contravention of the Charter in addition to being a Bill of Attainder. Consequently 194 should have been deemed unconstitutional on two counts.

Most thinking Palestinians realized that Israel could never give in on this issue. But Palestinian leadership also could not give in on the *right of return* as long as so many Palestinians lived in refugee camps. Their constituencies would not permit it. Behind the scenes diplomacy determined that the solution was to make the refugee problem a non-issue.

Alleviating the predicament of the Palestinian people replaced the problem of Palestine as a focus of concern. The West's growing independence from Persian Gulf oil was an enabling factor. The first step was the weakening of the hinterland of Palestinian militancy. This was achieved in several ways:

- The myth of Gaza's population density was finally dispelled. It was noted that Gaza was two thirds the size of Singapore with only half the population. The EU initiated the Gaza Project – dedicated to copying the Singapore development model. UNRWA (the sustainer of suffering and conflict) was dissolved and handling of the Palestinian refugees was transferred to the UN High Commission on Refugees. As a result all international law and codes of practice that had been applied to every other refugee problem now also applied to the Palestinians. The international dynamic became to resolve the plight of the refugees not to sustain it.

- About 250,000 Palestinian refugees remained in Lebanon. Their camps were more internment than refugee camps. Unlike Jordan the Lebanese did not permit Palestinian integration into the economy. The Palestinians were not citizens and had no rights (in contravention of international conventions and protocols on refugees). They lived in squalor with no hope of a better future.

They were therefore the most radical of all the Palestinian communities regarding the *right of return*. They were also excellent candidates for terror recruitment. EU and American pressure was put on Lebanon to end their discriminatory policy. The Lebanese were forced to grant refugees all the constitutional protections and rights granted to Lebanese citizens. An economic incentive was added. The refugee camps were given 'free port' status by the EU. Significant economic improvement in their situation followed. This benefited all Lebanese society. This branch of Palestinian militancy was neutralized.

- In 2007 the European Union and the United States joined in a project to generate a 10% yearly economic growth rate in Jordan over a period of 10 years. 60% of Jordan's citizens were Palestinian and they constituted the largest refugee population. Jordan's population was 90% literate with over 15% of their population possessing a post-high school education. Economically they were part of the undeveloped world but sociologically they were part of the developed world. They had the human resources to support a high growth rate and to become a modern middle class society relatively quickly. This project, along with other steps, eliminated the refugee problem in Jordan and lessened grassroots pressure on the Palestinian leadership regarding the *right of return*. This branch of Palestinian militancy was also neutralized.

- Israeli industrialist Stef Wertheimer initiated a project to build industrial parks in refugee camps within the Palestinian Authority. He was supported in this by the EU (which exerted pressure on the PA to cooperate). The EU gave these industrial parks a status equivalent to Israel's economic agreements with the EU. This parity stimulated international investment and rapid development. These camps have become modern well run towns and cities. The United States and Canada granted them similar access to their markets. Within 10 years residents of the Palestinian Authority had become middle class. Another branch of Palestinian militancy was neutralized.

- The United States "encouraged" Kuwait, the United Arab Emirates and Qatar to evolve into a Hong Kong/Taiwan development model. This would be a model for the rest of the Arab and Moslem world. They were offered defense agreements contingent on pursuing this path and not continuing to depend primarily on petrodollars. The success of the Energy Project and the liberation of the world from OPEC oil had made such a course of action economically imperative for these countries. It also made America's military presence not obligatory. Since their very physical existence depended on the American security umbrella they succumbed to American pressure – especially as the younger generation of leaders in these countries recognized the urgency of the economic imperative. This development model required a larger domestic population. Significant immigration from Jordan and Egypt was encouraged. Each country committed to absorbing 250 immigrants a day each from Jordan and Egypt respectively. Within 5 years over a million Jordanians (most of them Palestinians) and a million Egyptians had become permanent residents of these countries. As a consequence, the Hashemite component of the Jordanian population surpassed the Palestinian and because of the Jordanian development project described above the standard of living of both Hashemites and Palestinians improved significantly. An additional branch of Palestinian militancy was neutralized.

- Israel embarked on an educational affirmative action policy among Israeli Arabs – especially amongst women. The subsequent decrease in the size of Arab families because of the improved status of women generated a significant improvement in their standard of living (within the next decade it should equal that of the Jewish population). This has neutralized militant tendencies within the Israeli Arab community.

• The end of petrodollar power and modernizing trends in the Middle East led to the collapse of the Assad regime. Its successors required massive foreign aid from the US and EU. This was made contingent on the Syrians giving full citizenship to Palestinian refugees in Syria and the closing of all the Palestinian terror organizations. The last branch of Palestinian militancy was neutralized.

These developments made the *right of return* of Palestinian refugees a non-issue – removing Israel's greatest fear. Improved governance and the steady rise in the standard of living in the Palestinian Authority was a significant factor in dampening Palestinian militancy. This, along with the growing fatigue with the Palestinian question in the West and in the Arab world forced Palestinian leadership into a more practical mode. When the *Benelux Confederation Model* (Israel, Jordan and PA) was broached they became its most vigorous supporter.

NEUTRALIZING THE SETTLER PROBLEM

In 2007 there were about 300,000 Jewish settlers living in the West Bank. About 250,000 of them were living on 2% of the West Bank land that was contiguous to Israel proper. At Camp David and in subsequent negotiations the Palestinians had already agreed in principle that these areas could be annexed to Israel in return for an equal area of land from Israel contiguous to the Gaza strip. An alternative land trade came to be seen as more practical from the point of view of Israeli public opinion. The Gaza Strip would expand into Egypt and Egypt would receive a strip of land from Israel along the southern border of the Negev desert. The Egyptians did not reject this possibility out of hand.

The problem was therefore limited to about 60,000 settlers living west of the Defense Barrier. It was well known at the time that many would be willing to leave their homes if they were properly compensated. Many were in desperate economic straits, unable to make a living and unable to afford to move.

No Israeli government was politically capable of financing such a step. The United States would also have found it politically difficult to establish a fund for this purpose. But the European Union had no problem in this regard. They established a special fund and by 2010 over 20,000 settlers had been helped to relocate. The Israeli Government succumbed to combined US and EU pressure to stop building or expanding settlements. This process eroded the number of settlers west of the Barrier. By 2015 they numbered fewer than in Gaza during the 2005 disengagement. The final withdrawal in 2018 was less traumatic than predicted.

ISRAEL-SYRIAN PEACEMAKING

During Ehud Barak's premiership (1999-2001) Israel and Syria had been close to a peace agreement. It entailed Israel giving up the entire Golan Heights in return for a full peace agreement with Syria (and by implication Lebanon). This was the Land for Peace principle enshrined in United Nations decisions 242 and 338.

But the deal fell through. Not because of land but because of water. The Syrians wanted the border to be on the water's edge of the Sea of Galilee (the 1948 ceasefire and pre Six Day War border).

The Israelis wanted the border to be 300 yards from the waters edge (the 1947 partition plan border) because the Sea of Galilee is Israel's largest water reservoir and as such has great strategic value. The Israelis were afraid that, despite a peace treaty, Syrian dissidents or terrorists would attempt to poison this reservoir with biological or chemical weapons and bring Israel to its knees.

In 2008 this fear was neutralized in the following way. Israel gave up the entire Golan Heights (to water's edge) in return for a major European financed desalinization project designed to supply all the fresh water needs of Israel's coastal plain and the Gaza Strip. This did not prejudice any of Israel's rights to the water of the Sea. Israel became a major net gainer in its water resources; it gained a strategic water reserve in case of sabotage and most of all it had a peace agreement with Syria and Lebanon. Syria received the Golan Heights and agreed to close all Palestinian terror offices in Damascus and to cease being a conduit of Iranian arms to Hezbollah in Lebanon. Israel was the major beneficiary of this deal. Syria simply got back what the entire world thought was rightfully hers while Israel achieved strategic aims of profound importance.

ECONOMIC COOPERATION AS A BASIS FOR PEACE

Regional economic cooperation and mutual economic projects became the norm of all international aid. It was characterized by the highest level of cooperation between Europe and the United States since the end of the Cold War. The following regional projects were undertaken:

- The Tri-State Transshipment Project was based on projections for a doubling or tripling of EU—Asian trade by 2030 and the inadequacy of the Suez Canal to handle this increased traffic. The Red Sea Jordanian Port of Aqaba was selected to become one of the biggest container ports in the world, rivaling Singapore (the biggest transshipment port in the world in 2007). A rail line from Aqaba was built. Its route was through the Israeli side of the Arava, then along the Jordanian side of the Dead Sea and continuing on the Palestinian side of the Jordan Valley up to Beit Shean in Israel. Jericho became a gigantic warehousing and logistics staging area – employing Palestinians and Jordanians on both sides of the river – in which containers were unpacked and repacked. From Beit Shean the line continued by way of the Yizrael valley to the ports of Haifa, Ashdod and Gaza. The ports had to work on a 24/7 schedule. This forced the Israeli Ports Authority to hire large numbers of Israeli Arabs – since Jews could not work on the Sabbath and Jewish holidays. Peace with Lebanon and the subsequent availability of its ports made it a four nation project. The project created tens of thousands of well paying jobs for all four countries. Israel's multi-lingual society provided the project with an additional edge over other transshipment hubs – in addition to its favorable geographic location.

- The Dead Sea Development Authority was another tri-state project that included Israel, Jordan and Palestine. Israel did not have to give up any of its preexisting assets – not the hotels and not the Dead Sea Works. But all future expansion of the Dead Sea's economic potential (tourist and natural resources) was to be developed cooperatively with equal benefits for all three countries. The first thing on the agenda of the Authority was to reverse the catastrophic shrinking of the Dead Sea as a consequence of the diverting of normal water flow from the Jordan River. This was causing sinkholes that were threatening to swallow the hotels and the Dead Sea Works complex and prevented any significant subsequent development. Two projects were undertaken. They were made possible by the massive desalinization project that was part of the Syrian peace agreement. First, all diversion of normal water flow from the Jordan River was ended. Second, the direction of Israel's National Water Carrier was reversed. Seawater from the Mediterranean was pumped back up to an area adjacent to the Sea of Galilee and from there carried to the northern part of the Dead Sea by a newly constructed aqueduct. From the water level shrinking up to a meter a year in 2007 it is now rising.

- The Arava Agricultural Authority was a bi-state project that included Israel and Jordan. The entire Arava became a giant, fully automated agricultural plantation supplying fresh vegetables to Europe year round. Proceeds were divided equally between Jordan and Israel.

- The EU sponsored an expanded Orient Express. It began in Cairo and traveled along the coast of Sinai into Israel through Lebanon and Syria to Istanbul and from there to Paris. It became one of the tourist wonders of the world and helped stimulate a tourist explosion to the Middle East. It became one of the backbones of development and the biggest job creator in the region.

- The Tri-State Tourism Authority included Israel, Palestine and Jordan. Part of its development strategy was built on the Orient Express and it maintained active tourist cooperation with Syria and Egypt. Jerusalem, Bethlehem, the Dead Sea were all venues where jurisdiction overlapped and required cooperation. From two million foreign tourists a year to Israel/Palestine in 2006 over ten million now visit the holy land. Since every million tourists generates an additional 30,000 jobs this means that an additional 250,000 tourist jobs have been created. Moreover these jobs are now relatively well paid. Israeli social commentators had noted the dismal wages in the tourist sector and asserted that its expansion would have constituted an institutionalization of poverty in much the same way as labor intensive industries had done several generations earlier.

Agreement was reached between the *Histadrut*, the Government and the hotel sector. Wages would be doubled across the board. To offset the added expense and still keep prices competitive, property and other taxes were recognized as a deductible expense. These "lost" tax monies were made up by the taxes generated from economic activity stimulated by the increased buying power of such a large segment of the population.

- The Egyptian *Science City* in the northern Sinai was built with EU funding. At its center was the finest Polytechnic University in the Arab world. Its population was composed of technical academics that Egypt produced each year in numbers its economy could not absorb. It was a half hour trip by the new high speed rail line from Tel Aviv. Hundreds of Israeli high-tech companies built branches there and employ tens of thousands of Egyptian scientists and engineers. Today *Science City* not only sustains itself as a subcontractor to Israeli high-tech but has developed its own culture of innovation which is beginning to revolutionize Egyptian society in general. Perhaps more importantly tens of thousands of Egyptian intelligentsia are interacting daily with their Israeli counterparts on an equal basis. This group had been the most anti-peace constituency in the Arab world. Today they are at the forefront of creating a culture of peace in the Arab world. Instead of being the chief enemies of normalization, the Arab intelligentsia joined the Arab business classes in seeing its benefits.

- European Jewry helped fashion a wide coalition that made the *European-Mediterranean Free Trade Area* a reality. The *Free Trade Area* acted as a neutralizer to political and religious radicalism across the southern Mediterranean. It also enabled indirect relations between Israel and a half a dozen additional Arab countries.

THE DEMOCRATIZATION OF THE MOSLEM WORLD

The question that had troubled the world since 9/11 – can Islam become democratic? – was answered with a 'yes' and this reinforced the peace process described above. The demise of petrodollar power was essential to the process, since it forced the Moslem world to adapt to the norms of globalization. This process was accompanied by a clarification of terms and values on the part of the western democracies. What the West really wanted to spread around the world was constitutionalism. They realized that the theme of Fareed Zakaria's book *The Future of Freedom* (Norton, 2003) – that you must constitutionalize before you democratize – was essential unless you wanted to create monster regimes. The real question was what kind of democracy did you want – majoritarian or constitutional?

Majoritarianism places no limits on the will of the majority, or the leaders that speak in their name. Hitler, Stalin, Mao Tse Tung and Fidel Castro were 20th century examples of majoritarian rule. Hitler was elected in a democratic manner and was supported by the majority of the German people. There was little doubt that the majority of their respective peoples also supported Castro and Mao. Democratic elections in the Middle East had produced a fanatic regime in Algeria that resulted in a civil war that cost 200,000 lives and the election of *Hamas* in the Palestinian Authority.

Constitutionalism is the limitation of the powers of the sovereign in its dealings with the individual. The sovereign could be a King – as in England's constitutional monarchy – or it could be 'the people' – as in the constitutional republic of the United States. In both cases the rights of the individual are protected by a Bill of Rights against the arbitrary passions of an individual monarch or a majority of the people. The Constitution of the United States protects the individual from the majority and from the government that represents that majority.

To be effective it was necessary that the constitutionalism of Moslem countries be expressed in that part of the traditional language of Islam that sanctions and validates the inalienable rights of human beings created by God in His image. Islam has the cultural resources to provide this language. It is monotheistic and the monotheistic inheritance has given us two fundamental concepts without which democratic principles could not develop. The first is we are all made "in the image of God" and the second is we are all descendents of Adam and Eve.

During the Peasants Revolt in 14th century England one of the leaders of the Revolt queried: "if we are all descendents of Adam and Eve why should some be more privileged than others?" The biblical idea that we are all made "in the image of God" led these Englishmen to logically conclude that: "we are all equal in the eyes of God" and if we are all equal in the eyes of God why shouldn't we all be equal in the eyes of manmade law. These biblical concepts germinated in English culture until they received their full secular expression in the American Revolution and the Constitution of the United States.

Equality before God is inherent in all the monotheistic religions. Its most radical expression is the Moslem pilgrimage or *Haj* to Mecca. All the pilgrims are obliged to dress exactly alike so there is no differentiation between class, race or nation when they stand before God – because all are equal in the eyes of God. The *Haj*, joined with other Islamic traditions that define the inherent, inalienable rights of the individual enabled progressive Moslems to use their tradition to move Islam towards democracy. This was analogous to the founding fathers of the United States using the cultural constituents of their English forbearers – Common Law, Magna Carta, Petition of Right and the English Bill of Rights. One cultural asset of Islam that no other religion has is that its founder was a businessman and would have had little trouble with the globalized economy. Mohammed was a merchant and the economy of the Caliphate, when it was the most advanced civilization in the world, was a global economy.

What was still lacking in Islam was the secular western tradition of self-criticism and focus on the future that arose during the European Enlightenment. There was no Islamic Voltaire or Swift and there was too great a preoccupation with the past over the future. But self-criticism and the consequent focus on the future was the natural outcome of the initiatives described above. Joining the global economy required a focus on the future. In the early part of the 21st century many Moslem intellectuals (both Arab and non-Arab) had begun to address these deficiencies. Self-criticism and future oriented habits of thought, accessible and acceptable to the Moslem masses, by Moslem intellectuals and businessmen have generated a democratic transformation. This has been both a consequence of the peace process and a contributor to it. A New Middle East did not result from the Oslo Accords, but it is being built today.

CONCLUSION

P essimism had been the intellectual fashion in the late 20th and early 21st century. It reflected contempt for Enlightenment optimism. To be optimistic was to be naïve. It provoked condescension at best and hostility at worst. Today, however, it is optimism that is in fashion. To be pessimistic is to be shallow. It is indicative of a poverty of imagination, an inability to apply logical thought to the future. The optimistic human being is no longer a rarity – even amongst intellectuals and academics. Social commentators have called this *The Exodus from Pessimism*. The Jews were the collective Moses leading the way. The notion that the future is volitional is deeply rooted in Jewish tradition and reflected in the Talmudic concept *Ha'Reshoot Netuna* (it is up to us). It formed the backbone of the policies and projects described in previous chapters. We *imagineered* the future we desired and *engineered* our way to it.

PEACE

Peace in the Middle East was a consequence of this imagineering and engineering. Unapologetic Jewish self-esteem, a realistic evaluation of the political constraints of the globalized world and a proper respect for the legitimate positions of the Arab world combined to bring us to the point where we are today.

Peace has always been its own justification and needs no other sanction or rationale. Yet peace in the Middle East did have other constructive consequences, such as reinforcing trends of democratization in the Islamic world. Democratization moderated Arab nationalism. It encouraged an authentic culture of self-criticism.

The period known as *The Second Caliphate* dawned and the Arab world began developing like China after 1979 and India after 1991.

From 2010 until 2020 the countries of the Arab League sustained a 7-8% economic growth rate that was not dependent on oil but on goods and services. This forced them to depend on human not natural resources. Dependence on human resources in a globalized world of real time change required the empowerment of the individual which required an ongoing process of democratization.

Women had been the most misused and underemployed human resource in the Arab world. Their low status had long been recognized as a major factor in the backwardness of the Arab world. Their development now became a keystone of Arab development. Gender apartheid became defunct in the Moslem world and women became a primary development resource. Israeli Arab women especially became an example for their sisters across the Middle East.

ISRAELI ARABS

The leap from medievalism to modernity was exemplified in a television documentary about the Israeli Bedouin. It focused on a family in the Israeli Bedouin town of Rahat – some 30 kilometers north of Beersheba. Following is a précis of the documentary.

The family lives in a two story villa with 200 meters of living space, complete with every modern amenity. The father is a mathematics teacher who augments his income by translating educational computer games into Arabic. The mother is a nurse at Soroka Hospital. They have three children – one boy and two girls. The boy has just finished his MBA while working in the marketing department of an Israeli High Tech firm – writing promotional material in Arabic. In anticipation of his father retiring from teaching he has given notice to his employers. He intends to expand his father's small translation practice into a dynamic export company to other Middle Eastern countries. The eldest girl is an eye doctor – specializing in eye diseases common to the Middle East.

The youngest daughter has just finished her first degree in architecture and is applying for graduate studies at MIT. The family has a traditional Bedouin tent on their front lawn which they use to receive guests in the traditional way – before retiring to the house. In many ways it is similar to the Jewish custom of constructing a *Succah* at the Jewish holiday of *Succoth* (to memorialize the booths that the children of Israel constructed every night during their 40 years in the desert during the Exodus from Egypt). The difference being that the tent is a permanent fixture.

Rahat has three major economic branches. The first is tourism. The town has several 3 star hotels and dozens of Bed and Breakfasts with adjacent models of traditional Bedouin encampments. Families come from around the world to experience the Bedouin way of life. The Bedouin are openly contemptuous of anthropologists and other academics who criticize this commercialization of Bedouin tradition.

The second is architectural consulting based on Bedouin tent ventilation principles as a model for creating energy efficient buildings. These principles were first used by New York based Israeli architect Eli Attia in designing the famous Crystal Cathedral in Los Angeles (for Johnson and Burgee Architects). Bedouin architects have formed partnerships with Jewish firms and this service has become a major Israeli export. The third is translation and localization services of various kinds. In addition, many individual Bedouin have become desert scientists – combining the considerable empirical knowledge acquired from their tradition with the methods and mathematics of modern science.

The film deals with all these aspects.

RELIGIOUS JEWS

In Israel, peace liberated Religious Zionism from its fixation with the occupied territories. Following the withdrawal from the territories two factions evolved out of *Gush Emunim*: the melancholy faction and the *Tikkun Olam* faction. The *Tikkun Olam* faction took the energy and idealism that had been devoted to the territories and applied it to solving problems preoccupying Israel and the world. They became major players in re-branding Israel as the bridge between the developed and the developing worlds and played a disproportionate role in projects described in previous chapters. This transformation was compared to the industrial revolution in Japan when the energy and idealism of the *Samurai* tradition was transformed from a warrior ethos into an economic development ethos.

Initially the settler movement underwent an understandable period of dismay and spiritual desperation. But the majority chose to redefine themselves and to try to renovate their historical mission within the context of *Tikkun Olam*. This was to the benefit of Zionism and Jewish culture in general.

The original self defined mission of religious Zionism had been to be a uniting force in Jewish life: a bridge between the past and the future, between secular and religious and between the political right and political left. They had fulfilled this mission with considerable success before they became obsessed with the territories. This obsession caused them to be a divisive force in Jewish life, alienating secular Jews from tradition and isolating territorial moderates from the Zionist discussion. They had forced Israeli public discourse to be so preoccupied with the territories (pro or con) that it left room for little else.

In 2006 a study made by the American Jewish Committee found that 70% of American Jewish young people no longer saw Israel as a vital component of their Jewish identity. It concluded that Israel's preoccupation with its own internal debate had caused it to neglect formulating a new paradigm for relations with the Diaspora. Such a paradigm should, of necessity, include an updated version of the social idealism that had characterized the founders of the State – one that would inspire young Jews around the world to cultivate Jewish ambitions. 2008 was the turning point. The projects and initiatives described in previous chapters created a new paradigm of Israel-Diaspora relations and an updated version of Zionist social idealism. The practical pursuit of peace and the peace arrangements that were its consequence reinforced these developments and prodded religious Zionists into reinventing themselves in the image of their original mission.

ULTRA-ORTHODOX JEWS

The ultra-Orthodox (*Haredim*) in Israel went through a similar transformation. They realized that unless they joined the general society and economy their poverty would deepen, resentment against them would widen and their impact on the cultural values of Israel and the non-Orthodox Diaspora would be increasingly insignificant. A new generation of forward looking young Rabbis, born and raised in post-State Israel, issued a series of *Psakim* (Rabbinical decisions). The theme of these *Psakim* was that *Haredi* men in particular were obligated to take a major role in supporting their families economically, as was the case in the Diaspora.

Two factors were enlisted in making this argument. First were the arguments of the *Rambam*, known to the world as Moses Maimonides of whom it was said "from Moses to Moses there was none like Moses". He is generally considered the greatest Rabbi of the rabbinical era of Judaism. He believed that a Jew should not make his living from religious pursuits or study. Second was the realization that 80% of adult *Haredi* men not working tarnished the image of the entire community in the eyes of many Israelis and put religious practice itself in a negative light. The situation in their opinion constituted a *Hillul Ha'Shem* (transgression against God) and had to change.

This attitude, joined with opportunities opened up by the Internet, enabled a social revolution in the community. Both men and women could now become part of the global economy without compromising their traditional values. Working from their homes or communal communications centers they could plan their work day according to flexible hours. The men could attend Yeshiva and the women could attend to home and children and both could also devote several hours a day to making a living.

The *Haredim* became an important human resource in Israel's drive to become a global player in non-tangible exports. They were disproportionately represented in translation services, graphics, animation and the development of computerized educational games as well as dozens of other professions facilitated by the development of the Internet. As Israeli futurist, Rabbi Dr. Moshe Dror, had pointed out the Talmud page and the non-linear methods of finding information characteristic of Yeshiva studies were analogous to the methods used to surf the Internet. It was as if Yeshiva culture had been pre-adapted to the Internet age and the Haredim took to it like fish to water. Companies employing or outsourcing to Haredim advertised it and thus gained a certain qualitative distinction in the world market. Over 60% of Haredi adults are now in the work force – up from less than 40% in 2007. The tensions and resentments that had characterized the relations between secular and Haredi Jews in Israel have all but disappeared. They have become fully integrated and respected members of Israeli society.

European Jewry

The revitalization of European Jewry has been impressive over the past decade. At the beginning of the 21st century few had been optimistic about its prospects. Almost every discussion about the future of European Jewry was pessimistic. Its recovery is testament to the practical power of envisioning optimistic alternative futures in areas that ostensibly have nothing to do with the Jews.

The renewal began with the *African Sugarcane Project*, an offshoot of the *Jewish Energy Project*. In 2008 it was decided that European Jewish contributions intended for Israel be diverted to developing several large sugar cane plantations in equatorial Africa dedicated to producing ethanol as an additive to gasoline. This would reduce dependence on OPEC (and indirect financing of terror), help ameliorate African poverty and be good for the environment. Sugar cane was 8 times more efficient than corn as a food stock for ethanol.

The organized European Jewish community joined with environmentalists and European citizens of African descent to lobby for mandating the *immediate* universal use of E10, a blend of 90% gasoline and 10% ethanol. It is a high-octane, clean-burning fuel approved for use by all major car makers. It required no new infrastructure. Tanks, pumps, lines, and dispensers that were in current use for gasoline could be used for E10 ethanol blends without any modification. Conventional refineries could easily produce it.

The universal application of E10 in Europe saved the equivalent of 500,000 barrels of oil a day. When the United States and Canada adopted the same policy they saved close to the equivalent of one million barrels of oil a day. Japan and the rest of the world adopted the same policy and by 2010 the equivalent of over three million barrels of oil a day was being saved by this step alone. This exceeded the entire export of Iran and thus helped the West impose its reverse oil boycott on Iran.

This new lobby caused the EU to mandate flex fuel engines capable of using E85 (85% ethanol and 15% gasoline) for all new cars. When the rest of the world followed suit it resulted in the saving of the equivalent of 2 million barrels daily consumption each year for the past twelve years (a total savings of 24 million barrels of daily consumption).

Profits earned by the project were used to maintain boarding schools for African AIDS orphans. Celebrities such as Bono and Richard Branson were asked to serve on the Board of the Project. Bono's interest in alleviating African poverty and Branson's interest in alternative energy made them natural allies.

The planning and construction of the plantations was executed by Israeli companies. Agricultural equipment, fertilizers and insecticides were bought from Israeli companies. As a consequence Israel's economy benefited more than if the money had been donated directly to Israel.

The imagination of a project that was good for the environment, alleviated African poverty, helped AIDS orphans, indirectly undermined terror funding and still managed to contribute to the Israeli economy generated a great deal of enthusiasm. Previously unaffiliated Jews re-identified with the community. A European branch of *Ruth* was established and non-Jewish spouses of mixed marriages sought ways to identify with the Jewish community. *The Society for Humanistic Judaism* became the framework of choice to identify with the Jewish people. This was especially true among young people looking for a meaningful way of life and who discovered that in their past they had a Jewish ancestor. The humanistic Jewish option was more in keeping with the European Enlightenment tradition.

THE JEWS IN 2040

From the perspective of 2020 we can take pride in what the Jewish people have accomplished since 2007. But a vigorous civilization should never be satisfied with past accomplishments. It must always formulate ever greater visions of the future if it is to sustain its vigor and maintain its relevance.

Self-actualization and self-transcendence are the eternal challenges of the human condition. They are the essence of what it means to be human and must be addressed by every generation in its own way. This is especially true of the Jews. If Jewish history reveals anything it is this fact. Jewish culture is never as dynamic as when it is touching the nerve endings of the general human condition. This is the eternal truth of Jewish history – from antiquity when the Hebrew community discovered Monotheism to the Enlightenment, when Jews as individuals made discoveries, had insights and created ways of economic and social interaction that changed the course of civilization.

How is it that this numerically insignificant people has had and still has such an impact on society at large? How is it that one hundredth of one percent of the human race produces 30% of its Nobel Prize winners? Why is it that a country smaller than New Jersey in area and population preoccupies the world to the degree that it does? The answer I believe lies in a Jewish attitude towards life that is beyond doctrine or tradition. An attitude that is more sociological and psychological than philosophical. All Eastern philosophy and much of Western philosophy have been concerned with achieving equanimity, composure and tranquility in the face of the absurdity of existence. The Jews, on the other hand, seem to thrive in an attitude of never-ending dissatisfaction. We are never content; we are always looking for new ways to do things, to correct things (*Tikkun Olam*).

More than the people of the book we are the people of the eternal question. "Why?" and "why not?" are our two guiding lights.

We are the people who constantly question God, challenge God and wrestle with God. It is our never-ending questioning and challenging that has produced our contribution to humanity at large. It has probably also contributed to anti-Semitic attitudes. Many people are annoyed by an entire culture that is querulous. Being querulous can be dangerous. Just ask Socrates. Just ask the Jews.

The purpose of Zionism was to enable us to explore our uniqueness without suffering constant physical threats. We were to accomplish this by becoming like the *goyim* in terms of our *external characteristics* (the framework of a State defended by a powerful army). Zionism was not meant to turn us into a nation like other nations in terms of our *internal characteristics*. It was meant to provide us with a secure framework in which to pursue our uniqueness, not to encourage us to become like everybody else. It was meant to be an instrument with which to confront the future with certainty and security, *not to idolatrize the past*. It has performed this task.

We have neutralized all external threats and have successfully addressed the internal demographic threat. For the first time since Hitler Jewish populations worldwide are growing and the median age of the Jewish people is declining. We have ameliorated the demographic peril by way of imaginative undertakings designed to counter external threats. We can now in 2020 say, for the first time in over three thousand years that the physical survival of the Jewish people is assured. *Now what?*

What cultural edifice shall we build on this foundation of physical security? From the vantage point of 2020 it appears that the entire history of the Jewish people until now has been but an introduction, a preparation for our true task. The body of our collective book of life remains to be written. We have never been in this position before.

All the conditions – both Jewish and universal – are in place and amenable to the Jewish people fulfilling its universal potential. That of which the prophets spoke we can now do and if we do not we sin against ourselves and our history.

What is to be the organizing principle of human civilization in the future? If we can work this out for ourselves as Jews we will be a blessing to the world.

Acknowledgements

This book is a follow up of my first book *Futurizing the Jews* (Praeger, 2003) co-authored with my friend and colleague Rabbi Dr. Moshe Dror. The book was my intellectual biography and a summation of 30 years of thinking and writing. It was however published as an academic monograph and as such earned only a limited readership amongst professional futurists. It was the Christian futurist, Jay Gary, who suggested that I write a new book accessible to the non-professional. The product of that suggestion lies before you.

As my dedication indicates the driving force behind me on this project has been my friend and business partner Micaela Ziv. Without her support and encouragement I would not have completed this work. Nor would I have produced it without the ardent support and involvement of my friend Bill Cohen. Both Micaela and Bill viewed this project as their own and contributed energy and passion throughout. I would also like to make special mention of Benjy Vulfson, Micaela's life partner, for his unwavering encouragement.

A recent acquaintance, Ms. Claudia Chaves, made valuable suggestions for the book. I look forward to future collaboration in our common endeavors.

In writing the book the faces of my four children - Yonit, Dori, Nati and Mor - were constantly before me. What kind of future were I and my generation bequeathing to them? What would be the nature of the communal identity we would be remembered for? All parents who love their children are futurists. My love for my children provided me with the energy to stick with the project. It goes without saying that there would be no book without my late parents Max and

Anne. I am increasingly aware of what part of them is in me and how I am the product of their character and fortitude.

I must also acknowledge the place that the Nessyahu family played in my life. Everything I am intellectually, as a Jew and as a Zionist is a result of my being "adopted" by them when I came to Israel. Mordechay, Yehudit and Haimie are all deceased now and this has left a hole in my life.

THE AUTHOR'S WORLDVIEW

To be coherent and clear, an essay or a book must have a transparent starting point. Who I am and what I have become is my starting point. I was born and educated in America and came to Israel in my early 20's – one day before the Six Day War. I became a Zionist not because of ideological conviction but because I fell in love with Israel and the potential of its people. My motivations for writing the book as well as the views expressed in it are derived from an intense feeling that there is something exceptional about Jewish peoplehood; that we betray our ancestors, ourselves and human history when we turn our backs on that exceptionality. I believe that the modern State of Israel is not only a framework to guarantee the physical survival of the Jewish people; it is also a vessel by which we can give modern expression to the energy, idealism and creativity that has characterized so much of Jewish history. I also believe that unless we strive to achieve this second aspect of Israel's mission we will not succeed in sustaining the first.

The book is a manifestation of a wider Jewish and Zionist vision which asserts that: *If Israel will not be a light unto the nations it will not be a light unto the Jews.* This was a view held by David Ben Gurion. It is also my view and is the *leitmotif* of the entire book.

A word on what I mean by optimism. I do not mean irrational cheerfulness. Optimists are serious people. They believe that to be rational is to be optimistic; that the rational application of human imagination and energy can solve problems, improve conditions and modify the direction of historical trends (modify, not reverse or prevent). Pessimism is irrational and amoral. It denies humanity's ability to take responsibility for its own destiny. For pessimists the future is fated and we can do nothing about it - a mysticism of despair.

Optimists can be skeptical, discontented and depressed about conditions, but as long as they believe it is within the power of human reason, willpower and energy to create a better future they will still be optimists. To be Jewish is to be optimistic. As worried, concerned and depressed as we may be about circumstances, to be a Jew means to believe in the future and our ability to alter it for the better. It is in the spirit of this Jewishness that I have written this book.

READING GROUP GUIDE

POSSIBLE DISCUSSION QUESTIONS

1. Would you agree with the author's thesis that globalization is particularly friendly to the Jewish people? What arguments might you use against this thesis?

2. Why is it important to differentiate between rights, needs and necessities? Relate this to the author's claim that the Jews have rights to the entire Land of Israel but their own subjective needs as well as objective political necessities forbid them from exercising this right.

3. Would you agree with the author that the future is always more important than the past? How would you relate this to his call to shed the Nation that Dwells Alone attitude to life?

4. Would you agree with the author's positive views on the Oslo accords? Relate to his particular points.

5. Do you think the author's reference to the Italian liberal nationalist Mazzini, in connection to the essence of Zionism, is useful? Especially in the context of his ecological analogy of mono-culturalism weakening human society.

6. Does the author make a convincing case regarding the exceptionality of American Jewry, or is he overdoing it?

7. What is your opinion of the author's stress on the Jewish individual as the key to a meaningful existence of the Jewish collective?

8. What are your views regarding the author's claim that western immigrants experience a dissonance, as they are searching for self-actualization while Israeli society in general is preoccupied with the more basic biological and safety needs?

9. What is your opinion of the author's view that classical Zionism is no longer relevant and that it has to be reinvented?

10. Do you believe that the Diaspora and especially the Israeli Diaspora can fulfill the radical role that the author advocates?

11. Would you agree with the author that the post 1967 settlements in the occupied territories are the worst thing that has ever happened to Zionism?

12. Do you think the author offers a solid basis for Arab-Jewish relations?

13. Discuss the future of Jewish-Christian relations based on the author's views. Do you believe he offers a solid basis for Jewish-Christian relations?

14. Do you find the author's analysis of Israeli culture credible?

15. Do you find his discussion of Jewish identity and Jewish community compelling?

16. Do you think the *Jewish Energy Project* is realistic? Why? Why not?

17. Would you agree that the upgrading of Israel is of central concern to all of world Jewry? Why? Why not?

18. Do you think that the author's proposals regarding *Hasbara* would be useful and/or doable?

19. Do you find the author's views on peacemaking practical or impractical? Explain your argument.

20. What do you think of the attempt to apply futurist thinking to Jewish issues?

PLEASE VISIT OUR WEBSITE
WWW.THEOPTIMISTICJEW.COM

In order to:

- Learn about Tsvi's lectures, workshops and seminars for missions in Israel, events in your communities and organizational conventions.
- Learn how to start a $1,000 club and create a new, more democratic, paradigm for supporting Israel, developing Israel's economy and absorbing immigration.

ABOUT THE AUTHOR

Tsvi Bisk is an American-Israeli futurist, social researcher and strategy planning consultant. He is the director of the *Center for Strategic Futurist Thinking* (www.futurist-thinking.co.il). He is co-author of *Futurizing the Jews* (Praeger Press, 2003) and has published over 100 articles and essays in Hebrew and English. He is a popular lecturer in both Hebrew and English in areas pertaining to Jewish and Israeli futures.